SERMON FROM THE COMPOST PILE

Seven Steps Toward
Creating An *Inner* Garden.

SERMON FROM THE COMPOST PILE

Seven Steps Toward
Creating An *Inner* Garden.

by Edward F. Sylvia

cover illustration by the author

edited by
Scottie Priesmeyer

STAIRCASE PRESS
TROY, ILLINOIS

Published by Staircase Press
P.O. Box 83
Troy, Illinois 62294
(618) 667-4574
(618) 667-0095 fax
First printing 2001

Cataloging-in-Publication Data

Sylvia, Edward F.
    Sermon from the compost pile : seven steps toward creating
an inner garden / by Edward F. Sylvia ; cover illustration by the
author ; edited by Scottie Priesmeyer.
        p.   cm.
    ISBN 0-9702527-0-6
    1. Gardening—Religious aspects—Christianity.   2. Gardening
in the Bible.   3. Cosmology.   4. Spiritual life.   I. Priesmeyer,
Scottie. II. Title.   III. Title: Seven steps toward creating an
inner garden.
    248—dc21   00-090668

This book is printed on acid-free paper. ∞

to Harvey Stevens
Clayton Priestnal
Kathrene Casebolt

Acknowledgements

I would first like to thank the God of heaven and earth for the gift of life itself. I still marvel over the fact that there is such a thing as "me."

Moving down the cosmic scale, I owe loving thanks to my wife, Susan, and that there is such a thing as "her." She had unwavering confidence in this project from the very start, read every draft and endured through all my good and bad days. It is because of her that my fragile ego held together throughout the project.

I would also like to thank a long-time family friend, Rita Winters Licata, for making valuable suggestions very early in the writing of this book.

Special thanks goes to Scottie Priesmeyer, whose technical as well as creative skills helped me add "flesh" to my ideas. She continually kept the pressure on me to add ever more details to this manuscript. I consider her my mentor.

Thanks also goes out to special friends Duane Beougher, Sue Burns and Reverend David Reinstra for their comments.

I owe an enormous debt of gratitude to all those who knew me very little, or not at all, yet took time out of their busy schedules to read the manuscript and allow their comments to be printed on the back cover. You have all helped give me valuable credibility.

Finally, I would like to use this space to apologize to everyone throughout my life who has ever suffered due to lapses in my spiritual development. Please accept this book as part of that apology.

TABLE OF CONTENTS

INTRODUCTION

We all exist in two worlds – one visible, the other invisible. Whether you call it the soul, spirit, the subconscious, or the mind, we all have a private little world. This world is just as important to us as the outer world. In fact, our inner world is even more important,* because it colors our view of the outer world. This is why two people can react differently to the same external event in the outer world, such as a farmer thanking God for a rainstorm, while a city dweller curses the rain for ruining the weekend plans.

We would not be able to lie, deceive others, or be a hypocrite, unless we could function under a dual dynamic and have the ability to separate outer appearance from our inner reality. When we observe

---

*If our inner world survives the death of our physical existence, as we are taught by the religions of the world, then I couldn't imagine anything that could have more value to us.

co-workers kissing-up to the boss or politicians kissing babies, our suspicions are roused. We suspect such people as having a *hidden* agenda, or some ulterior motive, because we have all instinctively learned how to keep up appearances, e.g., "When in Rome do as the Romans do." Through the years we have even invented sayings to help us keep wary of mere outer appearances, like, "You can't always judge a book by its cover," and, "Beauty is only skin deep."

Perhaps the most salient words ever uttered to present this duality of worlds for our edification were, "White man speak with forked-tongue."

In the works of literature or film this duality of character is designated as the *text* and the *subtext*. The text involves what a particular character is literally saying, while the subtext consists of all the clues a reader or audience is being given to reveal what the character really *intends*.

Our justice system most certainly acknowledges the reality of this inner/outer dynamic. For instance, it is not enough to know that someone has killed another person, we also need to find the *inner motive* behind the physical act to determine the true severity of the crime. Because only then can we judge whether the killing was murder, manslaughter, an accident, or done in self-defense.

We also use a dual system for judging distance between ourselves and others. There is the physical distance between two people, yet we can feel "close" or "far" from individuals depending upon our relationships. Same with time. Time drags on when we are bored and flies when we are having fun, despite the constant speed of the minute hand on the clock. So we experience time and space inwardly as well as physically!

Having a discrete inner reality also explains why a person, after having accumulated wealth and fame in the physical world, can still feel empty – that something is still missing inside. Money and riches never guarantee happiness nor does physical beauty assure one of finding true love, because these things only address one of our worlds.

This is why religious leaders, psychologists, and therapists who help people find wholeness and completeness in their lives stress the importance of developing the inner world.

The problem we all face is, it's hard to change something that we can't see. And unfortunately, *our inner world is mostly invisible to us.* The human eye cannot penetrate its mysteries. So, as important as it is to develop this inner world, we first need a method to clearly see into it – *as clearly as we can see the objects of the physical world!* That is why I've written this book – to share with you a most remarkable, even miraculous, way, to see clearly into this otherwise hidden world.

Having felt the need to develop my own inner world, I became interested in gardening. The planning, physical work, and the peace of being alone in the garden all helped me to regain some balance from the stress and artificiality of the modern world.

More importantly, I began to learn new things about myself, as I prepared the soil, planted the seeds, watched over the growing plants, and reaped the rewards of my labors. I somehow started to sense that the closeness I felt with my garden transcended even the physical closeness of my nose burying itself inside the petals of a Star Gazer lily. The relationship with my garden was slowly turning into a kind of "peculiar recognition." It strangely reminded me of myself. It was as though I was experiencing what was inside me, outside myself. When I looked out into my garden, I was actually looking into my spirit! A world that was so hidden from me seemed now to reveal itself in unending detail.

I have often been struck by how many gardening metaphors are used to describe psychological processes.

We *cultivate* our minds (to make them more *fertile*).
Our ideas *flower* and *bloom*.
We bear *fruit*.
We plant the *seeds* of ideas in other people's minds.
We *reap* what we *sow*.

Those are just a few of the gardening terms we borrow from the outer world to describe invisible processes taking place in our inner world.

I find this fascinating. Not so much that it displays the ingenuity of a poet, but that the processes of the physical world could ever be conceived as emulating psychological processes in the first place. AND WHY DO THEY WORK SO WELL!?

There is an insight here that goes beyond creative license. And, after having spent 25 years of my life studying symbolism, I am convinced that ancient civilizations such as the Sumerians, Egyptians and even the Greeks believed the outer and inner worlds mirrored each other – exactly.

This was no mere primitive pastime either, but a sophisticated and true science. According to the discoveries of Emanuel Swedenborg, an 18th century scientist, philosopher and theologian, the ancients considered the analogies between the outer and inner worlds as the science of all sciences! He called it the

Science of Correspondences.* And it was boiled down to a very simple but provocative formula – As *above, so below.* This meant that the physical processes of the visible world corresponded exactly to the invisible processes of man's inner world. In other words, both worlds evolve and manifest in the same way. So that if ancient philosophers wanted to discover the secrets of human mind, they merely had to observe the world of nature. And since they saw the garden as Nature in her most refined and perfected form, they believed that one's inner world should emulate a garden.

This is why the ancient Persian word for garden was *paradise.*

In ancient Hebrew Scriptures, humans were put in the Garden of Eden. It was in this garden that Adam and Eve had everything they could ever want or desire. It was a perfect world, a world of peace, abundance, and harmony. And just as important, a world without stress, conflict or tragedy.

Today, thousands of years later, many people still feel a strong relationship to the garden, a relationship that seems to transcend the physical need to grow food.

I know I speak for other gardeners when I say I feel a special kindredness and connection to Nature when I am walking in and among the tomatoes, carrots, pole beans, grape vines and fruit trees growing in the garden. There are even days I feel like I'm in heaven! Especially on those magical days when all my

*Most of the ideas for this book were inspired by the works of Emanuel Swedenborg. He claimed that legends, fables, parables and hieroglyphics were sophisticated methods for teaching eternal spiritual truth, rather than historical fact, and that this knowledge has all been but lost to the modern world. I have provided a source at the back of this book for anyone wishing to investigate these ideas further.

senses and pores are opened by the vernal heat of spring, allowing me to receive all of Nature's gifts to the very depth of my soul.

In the garden I am greeted by the smiles of flowers, the flitting of butterflies, and the waft of delightful fragrances. Here, I observe an inspiring diligence and a merry work ethic among the pollinating bees and singing birds – all encouraging me to do likewise, and not be afraid to open my heart. Because here I find balance and a belonging. This is why, if it is a healthy garden, all the secrets of living in true harmony are put on display for everyone to see.

Even the color green, the most dominant color of the plant world, is the most soothing and peaceful color to the human mind. Perhaps this is also why gardening is America's most popular pastime, with two out of every five people participating in this "holistic" hobby every year.

While I am not the first to find wisdom and insights to a better quality of life among the tomatoes and eggplants, the purpose of this book is to go deeper than ever before. To dig deeper with our trowels and shovels, in the hope of uncovering the most profound truths.

If the ancient Science of Correspondences is true, then proper gardening techniques will not only reveal techniques which can be applied to our spiritual growth, but that the hidden processes working within a compost pile can be harnessed to significantly *speed up* one's inner evolution, just as compost is used to speed up the progress and fertility of the worldly garden.

And something more. Something that will no doubt raise a lot of eyebrows and controversy. For if the physical world indeed is a mirror of our inner world, as the ancients believed, then the greatest test of this concept would be to apply it to the Seven Day Creation Story of Genesis – to determine if the steps leading to the creation of the Garden of Eden might also correspond to the steps that a person must take towards the creation of an inner or spiritual garden!

This book is about how to help us fill the inner emptiness and the void left by living in the modern world – with a thriving, flowering and fruitful inner garden. This is the cornucopia of ancient legend, because only an inner garden can hold an unlimited harvest. The inner garden is the Promised Land!

As above, so below. And just like the things in a worldly garden, the inner garden has similar needs. It must be watered and cultivated. It is a world in which we must always be on the lookout for invasive weeds and annoying pests.

The inner garden suffers through droughts, heat, cold and storms...then rewards us with peace and beauty.

I will now take you on a unique journey, back and forth between the two worlds we all live in. But not as mere cosmic amphibians. Our goal is to become cosmic gardeners.

So let's get going.

STEP ONE: LET THERE BE LIGHT

As a young boy I had no particular fondness for gardening. You may say I even detested it. I certainly hated to mow the lawn. And although I loved that my grandparents lived on a farm, when it came to giving them a hand with the harvesting of potatoes or the weeding of strawberries, I would usually give up after 30 minutes.

The only fond memory I have of gardening was sitting in a field of peas, eating them rather than helping in the harvest. As far as I was concerned, the whole enjoyment of raising crops was in the eating; however, any kind of gardening work was to be nullified and rendered void.

Somehow I gradually came out of this *void*. Or should I say, something entered into it. We've all seen a cartoon where a light bulb appears above someone's head, indicating that the person has been struck by some new idea. Well, that's how gardening came back into my life.

Just like in a cartoon, it came to me one day in a flash. A synapse between some neurons in my brain gave me the idea that nothing could be more sagacious than to buy some land and plant a huge garden. It was the late 1970s and the world had gone through the second oil embargo of that decade. I was sure the world was headed for some kind of disaster, because of our total dependence on fossil fuels. All of which helped me to embrace the natural or organic methods of gardening. I was determined to create the most healthy and fertile soil possible without being a drain to the world's limited resources. I wanted to leave a small patch of land better off than when I found it. So at the very center of this *flash of insight* of mine was to build a large compost pile.

All new things start this way. An inner light turns on. It is not the blinding light that causes the eyes to squint. But a light that opens the eyes wide – from within, and leaves you with a new evaluation of things. And it usually comes in to fill some void or need, or pull you out of some darkness concerning some subject matter. One day I am diddley-bopping through life, and the next, gardening takes on major importance. It's like a revelation. We recognize a superior option, a better alternative.

As I mentioned in the introduction to this book, two of every five Americans now garden in one form or another. That's more than any other pastime in America. In fact, more people now have gardens than during the days of the Second World War, when being patriotic meant growing a victory garden.

And the numbers keep growing.

Not all people choose to garden because some "light bulb" goes off in their head. Nor am I implying that it begins from some deeply felt spiritual experience.

Certainly those who have chosen organic or natural ways of gardening over chemical methods would claim that they have made an *enlightened* choice. But it can be a lot more subtle and gradual than that. By seeing the "light," nothing more is meant than *recognizing* some new *value*.

The important thing is that people who garden do it from some strong conviction that they will be improving the quality of their life - whether they do it for the soul or not. Some people are seeking superior quality in the nutritional value and taste of their food. Some want fresh produce from their own backyard, so they can be certain it is untainted by chemicals like Alamar, Sevin and Dursban (which are not easily washed off). Others feel they are doing something positive in the world by not being an additional drain on the world's food supplies and resources. Still others seek the healing process of the physical work of digging and planting in the outdoors, which reduces tension and exercises many unused muscles. And finally, some people just plain enjoy it.

In these hectic times where convenience is highly valued, it is much easier to buy all our produce than raise it ourselves. However, if we recognize that gardening can change our lives in so many beneficial ways, we will set aside the time to prepare the soil, plant the seeds, and cultivate the health-giving plants all the way through to harvest-time.

Likewise, when we discover how much spiritual growth can change our lives for the better, we will set aside the time to prepare ourselves to receive the seeds of higher ideas, and cultivate our souls to be more fruitful.

This is what is spiritually meant by "let there be

light" in the Seven Days Creation story of the Bible. For without new insights that can bring about more solid values and convictions, the "genesis" of the inner garden can not begin.

The "light" which gets the inner growing process started is the light of *understanding.* If you contemplate this idea for a while, you will easily conclude that understanding is just like eyesight - but on a higher level. This is why when we understand something, we say "I see." While eyesight guides us to maneuver around physical objects, understanding guides us safely past obstacles which can stand in the way of our spiritual paths, such as envy, deceit, revenge, and any other behavior recognized as a character fault.

This new influence and understanding becomes the light which begins to shine in our inner world, a world that now begins to emerge out of some relative obscurity and continues to grow and evolve into a wonderful, thriving garden (in much the same way that God created the physical world out of darkness).

So, we now have our first correspondences between the outer and inner gardens. The worldly garden cannot grow without *light,* just as the inner garden cannot grow without *understanding.* But in order to explain the necessity of a spiritual compost pile to enhance our inner growth, which is no doubt a rather odd notion, I will first have to demonstrate how organic gardening methods are also the best methods for our inner garden. To do this, I will show why spiritual ideals correspond to organic ideals – that Nature's wisdom is God's wisdom.

A spiritual ideal is one that promotes the most universal benefit possible. That is why to *love one's neighbor* and the *Golden Rule* are examples of spiritual ideals. Spiritual ideas represent higher ideals because in order to accomplish them we each have to rise above ourselves and take the highest view, and see the big picture, in order that our actions will be of benefit to all others. Nature too, has evolved into ever more complex and interrelated "living" partnerships. All life has evolved for the benefit of the ecosystem, and the ecosystem has evolved for the benefit of all life.

Both natural and spiritual evolution takes identical paths – the high road!

This acknowledgement brings with it a certain degree of *humility*. We cannot accept new ideas unless we are able to give up old ideas. We cannot expand our sphere of love towards others unless we rid ourselves of our more selfish motives. This is not always easy. But *humility is the only way you can create a compost pile for your inner garden.*

Just as with a real compost pile, which is made from old leaves, grass clippings, and other garden refuse, the inner compost pile is made from the refuse of old and inferior ideas. These ideas are broken down by processes analogous to those working in a real compost pile and reconstituted to help support the growth of newer and more dynamic concepts.

Nothing is wasted. The evolution of both the physical garden of the world and the inner garden of the mind rely on similar organic processes and techniques.

The purpose of a compost pile is to create *humus*. What's interesting about the word *humus* is that it shares the same Latin origin as the word *humility*. And while humus is a prerequisite for healthy plant growth, humility is a prerequisite for spiritual growth.

I will explain in much greater detail all about the miraculous processes that occur within an inner compost pile in later chapters, as well as the unique correspondences between humus and humility. All that's needed for now, in taking the first step, is that we recognize and embrace superior or higher ideals.

When we see the "light," the work of our inner garden can begin. In fact, the point at which each of us personally realizes that we can only become better persons by recognizing and embracing higher ideals is the point at which our inner spirit acquires a "green thumb."*

The next step in the evolution of our inner garden will involve *discernment.*

---

*It is interesting to note that the evolution of the human thumb gave man the special ability to grasp things. One's understanding gives man the special ability to grasp and discern higher ideas.

STEP TWO: SEPARATING THE WATERS

Gardens need water. The inner garden needs water as well. Remember the ancient formula, *as above, so below.*

But what could water possibly represent on a higher level? What new exalted meaning could be superimposed upon this already precious resource? In other words, what is the psychological equivalent to water? Without knowing what it is, we would be unable to properly determine why separating the waters is so important to the second stage of our inner garden's evolution.

In very ancient times water symbolized *Truth.* Why? Because they saw that the *physical* properties of water corresponded exactly to the *psychological* properties of Truth.* For instance, water quenches the thirst of the body, while truth quenches the thirst of

---

*It is important to point out that while symbolism can be subjective and different for various cultures, correspondences are an exact and objective science and deal with the universal similitudes between the physical and higher realms.

the soul. Put another way, water is refreshing to the body.

Truth is refreshing to the soul.

Without water the body dies. Without Truth the soul dies.

Water bathes and keeps the body clean.

Truth cleanses and purifies the soul. This dynamic between water and truth is also what lies behind the sacrament of Baptism. Perhaps this also explains why Ponce de Leon and his men failed to find the fountain of youth in Florida, after being told by the Indians that it was indeed there. The Indians may well have been talking over the explorers' heads – since it is *truth* which leads us to eternal life!

If we apply this higher, psychological meaning to the different manifestations of water in the physical world, we can obtain more insights about the secrets of our inner world.

Rain falls on the earth much like information falls on our senses. Rain also collects in lakes and oceans. Similarly, knowledge collects in our memory. Symbolically speaking, bodies of water can be used to represent one's body of knowledge.

But this ocean of information that one collects throughout life is just that, a pool of ideas. While having an extensive memory is extremely valuable, we should not confuse memory with intelligence. A parrot is not intelligent because it responds correctly to the commands of its owner. Nor is a high school or college student who learns only by rote. Unfortunately, being able to provide the correct answer at the right time is considered smart. A good memory, however, is the mere retrieval of data and "stuff."

A good analogy between memory and intelligence can be made with an old chest in the attic. Opening the chest and going through the various objects inside is similar to how we use our memory. However, if by going through the objects in the chest we discover that by arranging these items in a special way we can redecorate the downstairs den, that's much closer to using our intelligence.

Intelligence is how we *arrange* the information stored in our memory. But we can't arrange information unless we classify it. And we can't classify it without weighing it against the principles and values we have adopted. For instance, two different people looking into the same chest might want to do different things with it. While the original person wants to use the items inside to redecorate the den, another person might see it all as junk and want to throw it away.

This is what is meant by the *separating of the waters* on the second day of creation in the Scriptures. Once we have recognized some higher ideal to live by, we must next begin the process of sorting things out. That way, we can separate what's relevant to our lives and what's not from all the things we have crammed into our heads. Otherwise, we can drown in a deluge of data.

Psychologically, a flood represents being overwhelmed by information. The whole symbolic meaning behind the biblical story of Noah's Ark is that when people ignore their inner development, and reject higher ideals, their memory becomes so inundated with all kinds of trivial, useless, and unorganized information that the soul drowns in it all. People can wander (surf) aimlessly for hours at a time on the Internet.

The Ark (higher ideals) was built according God's instructions (spiritual lessons) to provide us with the proper values in order to help us rise above it all and remain buoyant in troubled waters. That we live in the "Information Age" allows us to experience first hand how easy it is to get overwhelmed by the flood of information we receive daily.

The same goes for the gardener. Once a person decides that gardening is important to the enrichment of one's life, he or she must next wade through an *ocean* of information as to the various gardening methods and techniques that are available.

When I first decided to garden, I read everything I could get my hands on. I subscribed to a half dozen or so gardening magazines and purchased several book-shelves worth of books. And I was amazed at all the different techniques.

There was raised-bed gardening. Intensive gardening. Companion planting. Vertical gardening. Gardening with chemicals. Natural and organic gardening. And even edible landscaping. Let me go over these methods with you in some detail to give you a better idea of the kinds of choices I had to make.

RAISED-BED GARDENING

This is a method by which you plant on soil that has been "mounded-up" instead of planting at the ground level. There are several advantages to using this technique. First of all, it gives you complete control over the soil that you can work with. You can use pure top soil to form the raised beds, or make your own mixture of soil, sand and compost.

Another advantage is that raised beds allow for better drainage to prevent rotting or diseases caused by saturated soils and standing water. Also, by arranging your raised beds in smaller sections between walking paths, the gardener is spared from stepping on the growing areas which can compact the soil, making it less hospitable for optimum root growth.

Finally, raised beds created in the form of smaller and more manageable squares or rectangles allows the gardener to plant more intensively.

INTENSIVE GARDENING

This method of gardening forgoes the practice of planting crops in long rows. Rather, the gardener uses smaller, wider "blocks" of ground. This allows plants to be bunched together more closely, making more efficient use of every inch of planting area. Watering and fertilizing, as well as all of a gardener's energy, can be concentrated into smaller areas.

*Square Foot Gardening** takes intensive gardening to its highest mathematical efficiency. Each garden area is measured out into square foot grids. Plants are then planted within these grids according to their space requirements. A mature bush zucchini would require an area equal to nine square feet. Cabbages would take up one square foot each. Four lettuce plants could be planted in a square foot of garden soil or as many as nine radishes.

*The technique of Square Foot Gardening was developed by Mel Bartholomew, whose book of the same title (Square Foot Gardening - Rodale Press ©1981), is one of the biggest selling garden books of all time.

The increased density of the garden plants in a given spot produces a living mulch which protects the ground from the summer sun's hot rays and helps to preserve soil moisture. When one plant is harvested, another is simply planted back in its place,* so that a bare piece of ground is never seen.

Intensive gardening can also confuse insect pests when the method of *Intercropping* is used, that is, planting different kinds of crops closely together. Insects usually zero-in on a particular family of plants. When plants of a single variety are planted in rows, insects can have a field-day. Planting a *variety* of crops in close proximity makes it much more difficult for insect problems to get out of hand.

COMPANION PLANTING

Companion planting takes even intercropping to another level as it not only takes advantage of planting a variety of plants more closely together, as in intensive gardening, but makes use of the knowledge of what plants are the most compatible growing next to each other. Bush beans like to grow with corn, celery and strawberries. Peas get along with broccoli, carrots and radishes. Sunflowers like cucumbers and pumpkins. Speaking of sunflowers, companion planting is one of the most aesthetically pleasing methods of gardening because it also makes use of the beneficial qualities of colorful, flowering annuals and perennials.

Certain combinations of plants not only promote

---

*The down side of this is that you need an additional growing area to keep your replacement seedlings - but that's why it's called intensive gardening.

the health and vigor of each other but can also help
defend each other from insect invasions and other
pests. Marigolds repel nematodes. Daffodils are poisonous
to mice and other rodents. Strategies in using pungent
plants like onions, and an assortment of herbs like
pennyroyal, yarrow and wormwood will repel insects.
Other crops provide distractions. Eggplants will lure
the Colorado potato beetle from the potato crop.
Nasturtiums will also lure insects from other crops.

VERTICAL GARDENING

This method allows gardeners to get the most out
of a small space by planting "up." Obviously, pole
beans, peas, vining tomatoes, brambles such as blackberries and raspberries, grapes and hardy kiwi are
naturals for this type of method. Structures for this
type of gardening include arbors, fences, trellises, and
pole tents. However, melons, squash, cucumbers and
smaller pumpkins can work, too, so long as they are
provided with strong enough supports. One year I
successively grew winter squash and cantaloupe on
an arbor. I used my wife's old pantyhose to form slings
to give extra support to the enlargening squash and
melons as they hung from their vertically trained vines.

If you were to grow potatoes in a tub or barrel,
filling them with new layers of soil or compost as they
grew, that would also be a form of vertical gardening.
Terrace gardening on hills and slopes or planting in
multi-leveled strawberry jars are yet two more ways
to take advantage of vertical gardening space.

EDIBLE LANDSCAPING

Once, when I was attending a flower show at the Missouri Botanical Garden in St. Louis, Missouri, and looking over some literature from the various gardening clubs in my area, a man at the table tried to be helpful by asking me what kind of gardening I was interested in.

I said, "Edible landscaping."

He looked at me with a prolonged stare. I immediately knew he had a picture in his head of me walking around my yard, taking big bites out of trees, shrubs and award-winning dahlias.

As strange as it may first sound, this is the method designed most after the Garden of Eden. After all, Adam and Eve merely had to reach out and pick beautiful flowers in one hand and delicious fruit and berries with the other. Edible landscaping is nothing more than mixing edible crops among the ornamentals in the landscape scheme. A flower bed might have rhubarb, asparagus and colorful kale planted between the daylilies, impatiens and pansies. A blueberry bush might find itself among the azaleas and hostas. Instead of maple or oak, the shade trees might be hickory nut or pecan. In fact, on a casual walk through such a "front yard," a visitor might not even notice anything strange, at least not until the host offered the guest a sandwich made from dandelion greens.

GARDENING WITH CHEMICALS

The development of artificial fertilizers first came about after incinerating plant material, when it was found that the residue consisted mainly of three items: nitrogen, phosphorous and potash (potassium). Various proportions and combinations among these three chemicals make up the bulk of today's artificial fertilizers, which are usually put into a soluble form that can be taken up *directly* by the plant. The soil is seen merely as a medium to provide an anchor for the plant's roots.

Chemical insecticides and herbicides are just plain nasty stuff. One must use extreme caution, such as being aware of wind direction and taking some precautions so as to avoid contact with the skin when using them. And those are just the chemicals which are considered "safe." Other, more potent chemicals, can only be applied by licensed farmers or professionals.

The advantage of using chemicals is that their benefits are immediate. Insects are killed on contact and plants send out a quick flush of new green growth soon after artificial solutions and amendments are applied. In the long run, however, soil loses its fertility and many of the chemicals get into the ground water and into the food chain. To add insult to injury, insect pests, vermin, and even weeds continually gain immunity to all these chemical strategies.

Even though some chemical companies are now moving towards genetic engineering, there are still many concerns being raised about the impact on the environment. The biggest challenge to these more sophisticated scientific strategies remains the same – that everything in the world of nature is *connected*. So when a change is made in one plant, an unexpected change can pop up somewhere else. As an example, if you design a potato plant to be poisonous to the Colorado potato beetle, a problem could develop if the pollen of the designer potato plant reacts with wild plants of the same botanical family. Insects other than the potato bug could eventually become affected – like butterflies.

NATURAL AND ORGANIC GARDENING

All natural methods of gardening take into account that everything in the natural world is connected and interrelated. And since no person is wise enough to understand all these complex relationships, the natural or organic gardener merely observes Nature for the appropriate course of action. Perhaps the biggest insight for the natural gardener was the discovery that Nature *feeds the soil, not the plant.* This is the whole purpose behind the compost pile and returning organic matter into the soil. The soil and its microorganisms have evolved over untold millions of years to prepare raw materials into the most beneficial form possible for the roots of plants. Furthermore, by following natural principles, no harm is done anywhere else in the complex and interrelated web of life.

These are a few of the choices I was faced with once I decided that gardening was something I wanted to do. I had finished cramming my brain with information and now I had to separate out one method from another in this ocean of material. Some of these methods, like gardening with chemicals and natural gardening, represented entirely conflicting *principles.*

So, the next step was to make a decision as to what *principles* were the most homogeneous to the original purpose of creating my garden in the first

place. The methods I finally chose were picked based
on the insights received from the light of the original
"light bulb" that went off inside my head. I wanted to
live in a way that was less of a burden on the world's
limited resources by producing some of the things that
I would consume (a "prosumer" as opposed to just a
consumer). I wanted to give back to the soil the fortunes
of its fertility and abundance through vigorous mulching
and composting. And finally, to leave a piece of land
in a better (and more beautiful) condition than when
I found it.

The important point to make here is that the choices
we make for our earthly gardens, or any other worldly
pursuit, come from the principles we lay down in our
inner garden. This is why it is so important that we
choose higher ideals over inferior ones. The highest
ideal being the one from which the greatest number
of people will benefit, as opposed to purely selfish
pursuits. When we choose spiritual principles we
apply organic gardening techniques to our inner world,
because the spiritual gardener wishes to do the greatest
good for the environment – not just grow the biggest
tomatoes on the block.

This is why "separating the waters" constitutes the
second step of our inner development. Water corresponds
to knowledge. Knowledge has to be separated out from
the less valuable information, just as water is distilled
from its impurities. During the distillation of water,
steam rises upwards in a manner similar to the mental
process of *discerning* higher ideals from all the heterogeneous information (dregs) that is contained in our
memory. By separating the waters, we can see our
way through a situation. Issues become more clear.

We can now put our feet on *firm ground.*

So, when the gardener chooses to create an inner garden based on having received some enlightenment, then sorts things out in his mind as to what's truly important to his inner life and what's not, he is ready for the third phase.

Dry land can appear.

We can now begin the work of soil preparation.

STEP THREE: DRY LAND.
BRING FORTH THE HERB.

Soil is the foundation from which a garden is built. So, too, the inner garden. But whereas one chooses a patch of soil for his earthly garden based on physical and natural considerations, the soil for the inner garden comes from spiritual considerations.

An ideal spot for an earthly garden would be one with good soil, good sun exposure and closeness to a water source (to connect a hose). The ideal place for an inner garden is where there are good intentions, enlightenment, and some connection to a source of truth (for continued inspiration).

When a person has chosen principles to live by, and knows how to discern them from less desirable ones, he is ready to prepare the ground for the inner garden.

The soil of one's inner garden is called *character*. This is where one now solidifies his principles and beliefs. In the inner garden, the principles one stands for become the ground one stands on. This is why "dry land" can only appear at this stage, after sorting things out or "separating the waters."

It is a universal truth that you build from the ground up. You can't build the first and second stories of a house without an adequate foundation. Similarly, in nature it is the soil which supports the plant and animal kingdoms. For this reason the organic gardener knows to feed the soil first, and it is why the spiritual gardener feeds his character first. Just as the condition of the earth's soil determines the kind of plant and animal life above it, so too, does the condition of one's character determine the quality of thoughts and actions of an individual.

We have now arrived at stage three. This is where the inner world of a person begins to make its appearance in the outer world (dry land appears). It can now show itself to others, for we tend to make our outer world conform (correspond) to the convictions of our inner world.

Creative writers have instinctively made use of the technique of showing the inner quality of a character through *corresponding* physical features in the environment the character dwells in. In the movie *The Wizard of Oz*, Dorothy, Toto, the Lion, Scarecrow and Tin Man are in a dark, spooky forest when the wicked witch's flying monkeys swoop down on them. This is also why in horror movies, monsters hang out in bogs, caves, graveyards and mostly come out at night. It is why children will draw a happy picture by putting a smile on the sun's face. As *above, so below.*

Since the principles we choose support and provide

the *ground* for our inner reality, it is only a matter of time that these principles will affect the ground under our earthly feet. Now...how can I put this diplomatically? People living in the city are no less capable of kindness than those living in the country, but having lived both in a big city and now the country, it seems that those living on concrete have a more hardened view of things. This is why people living in the same apartment complex may never talk to their neighbors. On the other hand, I have had complete strangers wave at me from their cars and trucks on the country roads. To me, the difference between these two lifestyles is that one is a more natural environment and the other is a lot more *artificial.*

People become more artificial when they remove themselves from Nature, because they cut themselves off from Her grand scheme. They begin to feel more isolated, less trusting and are forced to compete unnecessarily. In Nature, all things are mutually connected and supportive of each other.

These extremes show up in the soils where different gardening techniques are used as well. For example, not only are the principles between a gardener who uses artificial chemicals and fertilizers different from the gardener who uses natural methods, but the quality of the soils in their respective gardens and lawns will, over time, reflect these differences.

As a teenager back in the early 60s, I remember one family in the neighborhood who was particularly proud of their lawn. It was thick, green, and not a single weed could be found. Then, one year, their beautiful grass lawn mysteriously degenerated. The couple who owned the property couldn't understand why this had happened, after all, they had done every-thing right. They applied fertilizer and weed killer exactly according to the directions on the sides of the bags. What they (and I) didn't know back then was that soil is a "living organism." Their total reliance on artificial inputs was gradually killing-off the earthworms and soil microbes, which had evolved over millions of years for the precise purpose of maintaining the integrity of the soil.

Soil which has relied entirely on artificial fertilizers actually loses its fertility every year. It becomes lifeless. On the other hand, soil that is prepared by organic or natural methods, such as adding compost and humus, becomes more fertile and dynamic with each passing year.

Likewise, someone whose inner life is governed entirely by artificial principles becomes more spiritually dead over time.

Artificial Fertilizers & Mental Toxins

The garden holds many wonderful things for us to observe: The miracle of seeds growing into living plants. The change of the seasons and the return of spring each year. The intoxicating smell of humus-rich garden soil. And the reward of fresh tasting fruits and vegetables we raised ourselves. These things become all the more wonderful when we realize they can also allow us to behold an even more amazing world - the world of our spirit. Analogies between these two worlds can reveal spiritual truths and teach us universal lessons for living in harmony.

They can also give us insights to our mistakes. For instance, artificial fertilizers have the same effect on a garden as artificial principles have on one's psyche. Both have a toxic effect. But what is an artificial principle?

Artificial principles *all have a limited scope.* For
instance, when a business executive makes his decisions
based on increasing quarterly growth, he may keep the
stockholders temporarily happy but may not make the
decisions necessary for the company to compete into
the future (which is toxic to the company). Similarly,
when a stockholder's stock goes up because thousands
of workers had to be laid off, the scope of the economic
boon is diminished. When an individual embraces and
adopts artificial ideals, there is a reluctance to sacrifice
for the benefit of the whole, and one's good fortunes
will not be based on good fortunes coming to all others.
There is a failure to see the "big picture."

Artificial principles therefore have the same effect
on the soil of our character as artificial fertilizers have
on garden soil - an immediate positive result with negative long term consequences. Artificial chemicals take
the *life* out of the soil over time by creating an unfriendly
environment for earthworms and other beneficial
microbes. The activity of earthworms and soil microbes
corresponds to "living principles," or ideals we put into
action. Within our inner garden, artificial notions
kill-off living principles (principles to live by like the
Golden Rule) – just like artificial fertilizers and other
chemicals kill-off the life in the soil – by creating an
unfriendly environment for unselfish thoughts to
thrive in and produce "good works."

Remember, in the last chapter I mentioned that
water corresponds to *knowledge.* Artificial fertilizers are
first mixed with water before they can be put into the
ground. Similarly, when we adopt artificial ideals, we
mix them with all our other notions and put them
into the ground of our convictions. If our convictions

are poisoned by artificial ideals, such as putting all our
needs above those of others, then we become inflexible,
hardened, and reject new ideas. Our minds actually
become less fertile.

And it gets worse. Soil that has depended on artificial
supplements year after year, not only loses its fertility,
but its very structure is destroyed. When soil becomes
compacted and *hardened* it finally loses its ability to even
absorb and hold water, resulting in soil erosion.
Psychologically, when we can no longer absorb and
hold on to truth, the result is an erosion of our
character.

At moments when I have chosen artificiality over
some universal truth, put myself above others, or lose
my humility, I find that in some measure I actually
become hardened - much like Pharaoh in Exodus. In
this biblical story the Egyptian Pharaoh refuses God's
command to set the Israelites free. Psychologically,
when I reject higher truths, I hold my inner potentials
in subjugation, so that all my inner energies stay
devoted to some vainglorious end (building monuments
to myself). These energies (like the Israelites) make
their final escape to the Promised Land (our fulfilled
potentials) only after the parting of the sea (separating
higher ideals from lower ones allows *new land* to
appear before us).

As I mentioned above, when our inner landscape
becomes hardened, new ideas are no longer absorbed.
And that's only the half of it. Unfortunately, when we
reject truth (water), more is taken from us (character
erosion). Just as water erosion takes valuable soil with
it, the higher principles that we may have once entertained (those learned from parents, teachers and the

clergy) are washed away. This lesson is illustrated in
Christian Scriptures by the words:

*"I tell you, that to every one who has will more be given; but
from him who has not, even what he has will be taken away."*
(Lk. 19:26)

Nature teaches us that everything is in flux.
Nothing stays the same. Therefore, soil will either
be getting more fertile or more barren. A fertile inner
world keeps getting more productive, while a barren
inner world keeps getting more desolate. And since
God created man and woman to live in a dual world
of spirit and matter, the Bible makes much use of the
analogies between these worlds for our instruction –
like comparing soil conditions to one's inner character.

*"A sower went out to sow. And as he sowed, some seeds fell
along the path, and the birds came and devoured them. Other
seeds fell on rocky ground, where they had not much soil, and
immediately they sprang up, since they had no depth of soil,
but when the sun rose they were scorched; and since they had
no root they withered away."*
(Mt 13:3)

The beaten path illustrates how nothing new can
take root where only old thoughts are entertained,
or where people are inwardly hardened and shallow.
Similarly, gardeners are very careful not to step on the
soil in their growing areas and prevent the soil from
becoming compacted. Plus, they will also rely on rotating
crops in different parts of the garden, which is analogous
to being open to new experiences.

The analogies are endless, because every type
of soil and garden condition can correspond to, and,

therefore, illuminate the qualities of particular human traits. (The Bible sets a precedent for us to make use of this investigative tool.) For instance, another type of soil that presents a problem for the gardener is sandy soil. The physical structure of sand does not allow it to hold or absorb water (truth) either. However, unlike hardened clay soil, which lets water roll off the top, sandy soil allows water to seep right through it.

"And everyone who hears these words of mine and does not do them will be like a foolish man who built his house upon the sand..." (Mt 7:26)

Similarly, some people have problems discerning truth, even when others attempt to guide them. Nothing connects with them. Nothing adheres. An inner world that is composed of "loose principles" represents a person whose life is full of conflicting, heterogeneous notions. They can say one thing and do another. They change with the blowing wind (like the sands of a desert). These are people who are easily swayed by trends, which include the "current" fashionable religion, scientific theory, slogan, hair or clothes style - no matter how diametrically opposed some of these might be to previously held views. This is why we are not to build houses on sand. It is an unstable foundation.

One might take issue with me by saying that people who are always changing their views are open to new thinking and are simply evolving. But personal evolution is not simply jumping from one view to the next. It is a value system (as mentioned in Chapter 2) that arranges and organizes the knowledge and ideas in our inner world exactly as Nature evolves, by creating a more complex and highly organized web of *living* and *dynamic* relationships.

The more I garden, the more I am convinced that true spiritual growth is based on organic principles, principles that bind our personal beliefs into a coherent whole so that we can recognize the "big picture." Such principles would bind all people together and raise everybody "up." We can't reach heaven as a society if we try to build a tower using the raw materials of our artificial self-interests.

The building of the Tower of Babel is a story using the *language of correspondences* to demonstrate what happens to those who seek to reach heaven by artificial means. "Heaven" represents the place where we can find the ultimate happiness. The construction of the tower signifies the plans and strategies of a people to reach it. In this famous biblical story, the tower is constructed of *hand-hewn* stone. Hand-hewn means man-made or artificial, as opposed to using stones as they are found in nature (God made). Since minerals, rocks and stones come from the ground, they represent the principles of our inner world that support us in our activities. Therefore, in the story of the Tower of Babel, artificial principles were employed by these people to reach heaven.

Artificial principles are destined to crumble. Because like the inferior mortar used in the Tower of Babel, artificial principles are in themselves *divisive* to society, rather than the cement that holds or binds people together. So, we are taught in this biblical story to be careful of the principles we choose to find our ultimate happiness, because they become our building blocks – mined from the very ground of our *character.*

"Every kingdom divided against itself is laid waste, and house falls upon house."
(Lk 11:17)

Spiritual principles bring everything together in a harmonious way to reinforce, complement, and promote each other because they are living (organic) principles. As such, nature's evolution and organic life's *reciprocal cooperation* emulates the wisdom of spiritual laws on a vast theater for us all to see.

This power to organize things harmoniously is easily observed in natural gardening methods where organic matter is returned to the soil. When organic matter, such as old leaves, breaks down, it is reduced to its more elementary constituents. Furthermore, the action of rain on this organic material (humus) produces acids, which not only help in releasing new minerals into the soil but also produces a "glue," which combines with minerals in the ground in a particular way to form *soil aggregates.* In other words, all the different soil particles begin to "jell," making the ground spongy, flexible, more homogeneous, and more resilient to environmental stresses, such as temperature fluctuations, wind, drought, and rain.

It is my observation that individuals who let higher principles be their guide are less likely to become stressed-out or "unglued" in the face of extremely challenging events, such as divorce, the loss of a job or loved one, including all the stresses from the demands modern life puts on us. In fact, when we observe such rare people in action, we say they've got it "together." All true principles, such as those found in God's commandments or the Golden Rule, help bind* together all the things within a person's inner landscape. They promote an inner peace by placing things in their true perspective. Our lives are put back in order. Our inner ecosystem becomes a value system, making us more resilient to changes and challenges in our external environment.

To take advantage of these organic and universal forces for the betterment of our own inner gardens, we need to create organic matter of a different order to properly feed the soil of our character. We need to make *spiritual humus*.

THE SPIRITUAL COMPOST PILE

When I first began telling friends that I was writing a manuscript entitled *Sermon From The Compost Pile*, some couldn't refrain from giggling. It was an obvious attempt on my part to make use of the famous "Sermon On The Mount" from the Christian Scriptures. The humor of course was that instead of writing from a lofty position, I had chosen something considered quite earthy. After all, a compost pile was a place where kitchen garbage and even manure accumulated.

Not your average pulpit.

But if we are to believe the Bible, mankind started from a very lowly and unflattering position, for God created man from the lowly dust of the ground.

This has even more significance when we take into account that God gave humans both an outer and an inner world. God not only breathed oxygen into

*Religion comes from the Latin word ligare (as in the word ligament), which means to bind, bring together and unite.

mankind, but *spiritual life.* God not only formed our bodies out of the dust of the earth, but in a corresponding way, formed our inner life from spiritual principles (spiritual ground).

The only way I know to accept a spiritual life is through humility. This is why in many religious customs people acknowledge the Divine Being by either kneeling, bowing or lying prostrate, actions which put us nearer to the lowly ground!

In this way, when we lower ourselves before a supreme source of wisdom, God is able to come into our inner life and begin the process of helping us create an inner garden.

If God's true purpose is to give man eternal life, then it is man's inner world that God seeks to address. It is from our inner world that God wishes to command, "Let there be light." It is from our inner world that God truly seeks to help us separate higher ideals (waters) from more selfish ones: to love our neighbor, and be like the good Samaritan, so that character (dry land) can emerge. But this can only occur through humility. Humility is the humus which is created out of the spiritual compost pile.

"For every one who exalts himself will be humbled, and he who humbles himself will be exalted."
(Lk 14:11)

I have mentioned before that *humus* and *humility* come from the same Latin origin. Curiously, even the Latin word for man, homo, shares the same Latin origins. It is as though the Latin word for man was created out of the word "ground," much like God fashioned man out of the dust of the earth. It becomes even more interesting when one considers that the Hebrew word for ground and man is also the same – Adam!

People who have the humility to give up old ideas for new ones allow a power greater than themselves to raise their character out of the ground of new principles and breathe spiritual life into them. These people are true spiritual gardeners.

But old ideas die hard.

I've had to change a lot of my beliefs over the years, and it is a humbling, painful experience. The process itself can best be described as a slow *smoldering.*

One feels the heat at such challenging times.

One also feels heat when one reaches into a compost pile. The same universal processes are at work here. Just as old leaves are broken down and reconstituted in the compost pile, our old ideas are scrutinized and reconstituted under the organizing power of higher, more universal principles. Heat is generated by the friction between old and new ideas, and from our natural disposition to resist change or admit we were wrong.

Through humility an inner *homo*geneity is created within our character in the same manner that soil *aggregates* form through the action of humus.

Seeds and Plants

Once we choose the principles we want to live by as opposed to those we don't, we put our lives on solid ground. We have done the work of preparing our soil. Our inner garden is now ready for planting. We are ready to receive new ideas, nurture them, and let them grow within us.

Ideas are similar to seeds in every way. In fact, in our everyday language, we will use the expression "plant a seed" to suggest influencing someone with an idea.

Seeds have within them the whole blueprint for the plant that is to follow. Similarly, an idea contains within it the whole plan that is to be followed. An idea germinates into thought. The more ideas we have, the more our thoughts branch out.

Plants in the inner garden represent our thoughts and evolving perceptions. They represent the world of our intellect, and our understanding of things. Thoughts grow towards and seek enlightenment just like plants grow towards and absorb sunlight. As our ideas grow, they also represent more organized forms of the principles they are rooted in – the principles we have chosen which constitute our "ground."

Our thoughts exalt our principles just as plants exalt the mineral kingdom by taking minerals out of the ground and arranging them into more superior, organic forms. For instance, if I get an idea to do a good deed for someone, the resulting thoughts about how to best plan and accomplish the good deed raises the principle itself into a more superior form.

Principles "come alive," become more organic, through thought! One could say then, that the third stage of our development is the *greening* of our inner world.

MEDICINAL LEAVES AND HERBS

Fascinating research has been done on chimpanzees and their ability to find plants with particular chemical properties capable of curing particular illnesses. And, I suspect, eventually it will be discovered that other animals have the ability to recognize healing plants as well. I have personally observed dogs and cats chewing on grass to aid digestion.

One of the concerns for saving the tropical rain forests is not only their effect on climates and maintaining optimal oxygen/carbon dioxide levels but that a cure for such dreadful diseases as cancer may be found in the leaves of rapidly vanishing plants.

Close to 50% of all the medicines in the physician's arsenal to fight disease come from the plant kingdom. Penicillin was derived from the excretions of a common mold. The heart stimulant digitalis was derived from the lovely foxglove plant which can be seen growing in many perennial flower gardens. And aspirin was produced from naturally-occuring compounds found in the willow tree.

While once considered "occult-ish", herbal supplements have really taken off over the last several years and can now be found on the store shelves next to standard vitamins and minerals. And they seem to be taking up more of the shelf space every year! Garlic tablets are said to help bring down blood pressure. Ginseng increases strength and energy. Gingko enhances memory. Astragalus and Echinacea boost the immune system. Peppermint and Ginger settle the stomach and aid digestion. And Valerian Root promotes sleep, just to mention a few.

From the healing properties of herbs, we can gain another example of how our intellectual world corresponds to the plant kingdom. Thoughts have healing powers too! Thought and judgement helps us to filter out extraneous or discordant ideas and notions (clear the air) just as the plant kingdom filters and cleans the atmosphere of the planet.

Meditation, which is a very intense and concentrated form of thought, has been used to promote the well-being of *spirit* for thousands of years. More recently, books have appeared on the power of positive thinking. Thoughts are the "leafing-out" of belief systems. In spiritual terms, the flora within our inner garden represents our FAITH.* This is why the Tree of Life was originally growing in the center of the Garden of Eden:

"And out of the ground made Jehovah God to grow every tree desirable to behold, and good for food; the tree of lives also, in the <u>midst</u> of the garden..."　　(Gen. 2:9)

But when God's belief system no longer took a central role in man's life, the "tree of knowledge of good and evil" then took the central position in the garden.

"And the woman said unto the serpent, We may eat of the fruit of the tree of the garden; but of the fruit of the tree which is in the midst of the garden, God hath said, Ye shall not eat of it, neither shall ye touch it, lest ye die."
(Gen. 3:2)

When we choose ideas and foster notions that can be hurtful or detrimental to ourselves and others, our inner garden reflects noxious plants like thorn bushes, thistles, poison ivy and strangling vines.

"Thorns also and thistles shall it bring forth to thee;"
(Gen 3:18)

*It is said that Buddha worked out his method of salvation while meditating under a tree. In Hinduism, the sacred Asvattha Tree has its roots in heaven (spiritual principles) so that its branches (heavenly influences) can spread down towards man.

However, when our ideas grow into beneficial thoughts, they can serve as "food" and even as psychological curatives. Mental constructs are "food for thought", just as plants are food for the body. We "chew on" and "digest" information when we read books, or listen to the words of others, in the same way that our bodies take in food. And we do so to gain some beneficial result. By studying which plant or herb benefits what part of the body when it is consumed, we can form some conclusion as to what ideas are valuable to *corresponding* spiritual functions.

For instance, it is believed that the extract from milk thistle seed is good for the liver. The liver is responsible for removing impurities in the blood, which can corrupt the concord of the bodily kingdom. Therefore, the attributes of the compounds in milk thistle seeds must somehow offer the liver assistance in this most vital function. As *above, so below*. Likewise, if we wish to purify our inner spirit we must be willing to absorb the lessons which instruct us on the importance of keeping vigilance over and exposing discordant ideas like envy, deceit or selfishness that chance to enter our thoughts. Then, like a healthy liver, we are able to filter them out where they can be expelled from our inner life – as bile* is expelled into the gall bladder.

All healing herbs correspond to some particular *helpful instruction*. When we hunger for and seek knowledge, our *spirits* are doing something similar to animals that instinctively seek out plants for their special curative properties.

*Bile is a bitter greenish fluid secreted by the liver. Psychologically, it corresponds to someone in an ill-humored state.

FLOWERS

The ideas within our inner garden are at first like
tender sprouts. But they grow larger. Grow stronger.
Buds appear. Eventually they blossom, giving us a
feeling of new joy and gladness. Flowers are the plant
kingdom smiling at us; and when I stroll through a
garden that is bursting with different colored blooms,
I cannot help but smile back and be inspired.

The cause for this new joy is that flowers precede
the fruits, berries, nuts and seeds. Therefore, in our
inner garden they represent the excitement and joy
that comes as we *anticipate* some goal or result – the
new fruit of our labors. It is the kind of happiness that
bursts out as we find greater harmony and value in
unselfish work. The beauty of a flower is not appreciated
until its petals open. Similarly, the beauty in one's inner
garden comes from one's openness and acceptance of others.

Rarely do flowers in a garden clash with each
other. Rather, they complement each other's different
colors, shapes and sizes. When one's inner garden is in
full bloom there is an exhilarating sense of cooperation,
as opposed to the dehumanizing practice of cut-throat
competition, which pulls us all down to the level of a
mere commodity. We feel a part of and a oneness with
the grand plan of things because we are about to do
some greater good.

Flowers also can emit wonderful fragrances. Smells
correspond to qualities. Pleasant smells represent
environments which are appealing and promote good
will, such as when we are among close friends or cele-
brating special occasions with family. On the other

hand, offensive smells represent things which raise suspicion – such as something smelling "rotten" or "fishy." A situation "stinks" when people detect some unfairness taking place, and the culprit is often called a "skunk."

I have found the greatest happiness in my life while I was unselfishly contributing to some task or goal, especially alongside others – whether playing team sports or jumping in to help co-workers meet a deadline. And I can say this with the full experience of having tried all the selfish ways of finding happiness, such as playing politics, kissing-up to people, and yes, scheming against others. While this kind of strategy helped me to succeed in getting some raises and promotions, I was doing so in a "hell" of my own making – a hell that never left me satisfied.

The inner garden is an inner state. It is not some-place you go to. It is something you become. That is why happiness is a *choice*.

Fruit

Finally, our ideas do bear fruit. Fruit is delicious, and so too, can be the results of our labors. People around us can actually experience and partake of the sweetness that they perceive in our actions.

It is not uncommon to hear someone being called "sweet" because he or she acted in a very giving or thoughtful way, such as remembering a person with a simple note or card, letting someone get ahead of you at the grocery store check-out line, or returning a wallet found laying on the sidewalk. Women tend to use the expression "sweet" more than men, but men will buy chocolates and sweets to communicate a willingness to share their best inner qualities with another.

Both men and women will refer to each other as "honey" to indicate they find favor in the other's manifestations. When I was growing up, school children would still bring an apple to the teacher in a gesture of thankfulness for the lessons learned. When things have the opposite or detrimental effect on us we refer to them as going "sour." If we disapprove of a person's actions, we'll say he or she acted in bad taste. Fruit represents all the qualities of our inner world which we "ripen" or bring to completion. Good or bad, they are how we package ourselves to others – what we share with others. Our actions do leave a taste in people's mouths.

"Ye shall know them by their fruits."
(Mt 7:16)

"Bear fruits that befit repentance..."
(Lk 3:8)

"I chose you and appointed you that you should go and bear fruit..."
(John 15:16)

Fruit has another important feature. It not only brings enjoyment to our palates, but something that lies even deeper within – seeds! Similarly, within every act of goodness, lie the seeds that will affect the lives of others. It becomes contagious and spreads!

"Good works" go deeper than giving money to your favorite charity or running the PTA bake sale. They are selfless acts which can affect the inner garden of others. For instance, if you teach someone how to fish, cook, write, unlock their hidden potentials or improve their communication skills, you are not only helping to cultivate that person's inner garden, but you also make it possible for him or her to go out and spread similar valuable ideas to other people's inner gardens.

WEEDS

Weeds plague the inner as well as outer garden.

The best definition I've heard of a weed is that it is a plant growing in a place where you don't want it, such as goldenrod or shatter cane within the corn rows; pigweed competing with lettuce in the raised beds; or Canadian thistle among the melons.

Similarly, a weed in the spiritual garden is an inappropriate idea that sprouts up where you don't want it. This can be anything from daydreaming during an important business meeting, to having a vendetta against your neighbor across the street, to imagining you're God's gift to the world. Like weeds, these unproductive thoughts can rob energy from and choke off more noble thoughts. In fact, certain kinds of negative thinking can be so invasive as to completely take over our inner gardens. This happens when we become overly obsessed with negative news or constantly dwell on past disappointments.

This is why our inner garden must be constantly attended to. It doesn't take long before we find ourselves and our lives getting out of control because we allowed some inappropriate thoughts to sneak in and take hold. The trick is knowing which kinds of thoughts are weeds and which are worthy of our continued cultivation – which isn't always easy, especially if we rationalize our mistakes or think we're always in the right.

It all has to do with our *aim* or *intent* – the soil preparation we made for our inner gardens. Remember, a weed is a plant growing someplace where we don't want it. An unwanted idea sprouting up in our inner garden is one that is at odds with or heterogeneous to our guiding principles. When our thoughts are not firmly rooted in our principles, negative thoughts can easily emerge without detection. For instance, if I were only to give lip service to the idea of teamwork and good sportsmanship when playing in a basketball game, the sudden urge to "hog" the ball would not seem out of character with me in the heat of battle.

A person who has adopted definite principles to live by can recognize a good idea from a bad one as easily as a gardener can recognize a tomato plant from the stinging nettle weed. When we can identify what doesn't belong in our inner garden we can yank it out just like a weed in the earthly garden.

But false notions, as with weeds, don't have to be completely discarded. An insightful lesson can be learned from the organic or natural gardener who believes weeds can be turned useful to the garden when thrown back into the compost pile. Our negative thoughts and bad judgements can also be turned useful to our inner garden. It's called *learning from one's mistakes* – which is what happens when improper ideas are broken down under the scrutinizing and regenerative powers of the spiritual compost pile.

When we learn from our mistakes, psychological weeds find it difficult to take root again, or go to seed. It is otherwise when we depend on artificial methods for removing the weeds of our inner garden.

HERBICIDES & DRUGS

Herbicides like Atrazine, Diquat and Endothal

effectively kill weeds. The bottom line is that herbicides do nothing to benefit the soil. Plants, flowers and their fruit are a reflection of the quality of the soil, just like our thoughts, happiness and productivity is a reflection of the principles we stand for. That is why those who use natural gardening methods stay away from herbicides. They simply put the weeds in their compost pile or put a deep layer of mulch in their gardens to smother and keep the weeds down. Either way, the plant material of the weed goes back into the ground to increase soil fertility. While crops need fertile soils, many weeds actually prefer bad soils. So herbicides continue to render the soil more suitable for weed growth since they add nothing to soil fertility. Finally, weeds may become more resistant to the herbicides, and newer herbicides have to be developed.

There are methods of ridding oneself of negative thoughts that are similar to using herbicides. These are short-sighted and quick solutions which have an immediate effect, but do nothing to correct the under-lying problem.

Like herbicides, many of these solutions involve chemical dependence in one way or another. Alcohol and drugs produce an immediate effect of well-being. Their long term use can be disastrous. Alcohol clouds our judgement, causes fits of rage, and leads to the degeneration of our vital organs, like cirrhosis of the liver. Tranquilizers and "recreational" drugs, such as marijuana, cocaine and sedatives only put off our daily stresses, insecurities, and problems of low self-esteem. They keep us from reaching our evolutionary potentials that make us more valuable to society. Ironically, our self-worth is based on whether or not we feel we are a valuable part of society. In short, these methods do nothing to improve the soil of our inner garden, the only place which all good things can spring forth. Finally, like herbicides, these drugs lose their effect. Stronger doses have to be taken, or newer drugs have to be tried.

FERTILIZERS & EDUCATION

If herbicides correspond to artificial methods of eliminating negative thoughts, then chemical fertilizers, which feed the plant directly and not the soil, can be looked at as an artificial means for promoting our intellect. Modern education has become such a short-sighted method. Morality, ethics, and other issues of character are put aside so that kids can be put on the learning fast track. The mind is fed directly, without any character (soil) building. Proud is the parent whose child learns to read by three or play piano at age five. But every year newspaper articles give us embarrassing stories of very intelligent people being caught doing stupid things. Everyone should have some idea of what's right and wrong in society. We have laws of conduct that we must follow to become good citizens, and commandments to follow, if we want to be good citizens in the hereafter. However, if *conscience* is not affected in our learning years, these laws will have no real influence on our inner life or the soil of our character. Instead, we speed up our car when the police officer is seen far back in the rearview mirror, or we act immorally when a priest or minister is nowhere in sight – regardless of what our school test scores were.

"Beware of the leaven of the Pharisees, which is hypocrisy.
Nothing is covered up that will not be revealed, or hidden that
will not be known. Whatever you have said in the dark shall
be heard in the light, and what you have whispered in private
rooms shall be proclaimed upon the housetops."
(Lk 12:1,2,3)

Hypocrisy is nothing more than using codes of
conduct as an "artificial" means by which to appear
in a good light to others. Politicians kiss babies and
promise anything. The Pharisees used the pretense of
the holy temple in which to *make a fast buck.* Such
people use their knowledge and education to feed
their cleverness rather than character. It's like trying
to increase our intellectual capacity when the intent
(foundation) is all wrong.

Shortsighted solutions, like chemical solutions,
can therefore pollute every aspect of a spiritual garden
in the long run. As stewards of our inner gardens we
must realize that our good or bad thoughts sprout up
from something in our character. When we try to
rationalize our mistakes or blame others for all our
problems we throw down our spiritual garden spades
and hoes, and walk away from the true chores of the
inner garden.

"Why do you see the speck that is in your brother's eye,
but do not see the log that is in your own eye?"
(Mt 7:3)

There has been a trend over the last several
decades of people playing the part of the victim, blaming
others for their troubles and not taking responsibility
for their actions. As a result we have become a more
litigious society.

You reap what you sow. This is the Christian
equivalent of karma. It would not be so if our inner
nature was not an ecosystem corresponding exactly to
Mother Nature. Everything returns to its source, just
as leaves and seeds return to the very soil from which
they came. Likewise our ideas, thoughts and actions
all come back to the soil of our character to haunt us.
I call this our inner *ecological karma*. What goes
around comes around.

Having a spiritual compost pile comes from taking
responsibility for one's thoughts and actions, no
matter how painful or unflattering they may feel. If
the inner compost pile is humility, sincerity is the
pitch fork which turns everything over to let the air
get in.

Because of the daily vigilance required for the care
and upkeep of our inner gardens, additional help from
"above" is now needed.

We must continuously look upwards for a constant
source of inspiration.

1980 – No trees, no flowers, no worms. What have I gotten myself into?

1999 – Trees, flowers, worms and even deer.

Raised beds give you total control over the consistency and quality of the soil — you simply make your own mixture.

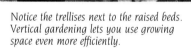

Notice the trellises next to the raised beds. Vertical gardening lets you use growing space even more efficiently.

Pea planter.

Pea picker!

Intensive gardening lets you place a variety of different garden plants closely together. As they grow, they will fill in all the spaces to create a moisture-saving living mulch.

Watering is much more efficient with raised beds.

All in the family — daughter Tara, Edward III and youngest son, Adam, all pitch in to harvest potatoes.

Adam and I are making
Apple Pie In A Jar.

Why buy flowers
when you can pick
them? By the way,
these daylilies are
edible.

Adam picks apples
while Bear Puff supervises.

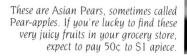

These are Asian Pears, sometimes called
Pear-apples. If you're lucky to find these
very juicy fruits in your grocery store,
expect to pay 50¢ to $1 apiece.

Roses and dahlias – don't worry,
I didn't eat these!

My very first hickory nut!

What do you get when you
cross a hazelnut with a filbert?
A hazelbert!

American Chestnuts.
This tree used to dominate the eastern
US forests until they were hit by a
blight in the early 1900's.
I'm proud to have one.

Two compost bins
are better than one!

In 1986 we raised
40 ducklings.

Why say "cheese" when you can say "pumpkin?"

To feed and attract birds throughout winter,
I use a birdfeeder and plant shrubs like
Winterberry, a deciduous holly.

This monarch butterfly is enjoying the
nectar from the Blue Mist shrub.

Over the years I've planted trees
and shrubs to give the garden color
all year round.

The praying mantis. This "pious" predator
kills its prey with a bite to the back of the head.

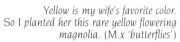

Yellow is my wife's favorite color.
So I planted her this rare yellow flowering
magnolia. (M.x 'butterflies')

When my wife wants flowers, I just tell her,
"you know where the scissors are!"

Beauty is hard work. That's me working behind the
scenes with my trusty wheelbarrow.

A one-in-a-million shot. It wasn't until this photo was developed that we realized Adam was pointing at two eyes instead of two dandelions.

Peaceful outside, peaceful within.

STEP FOUR: THE SUN, MOON
               AND THE STARS

There can be no garden without the sun, an energy source that we can count on every day. Likewise, we should not expect to create an inner garden without some continuous light source as well. You may be asking why, if we saw the "light" earlier, should we still be seeking a light source?

The answer to this question actually gives further support to the idea that the Seven Day Creation Story is actually a metaphor for the steps we must go through to create an inner garden – a paradise for the heart and mind. Some people believe in the literal sense of the creation story as a matter of faith. But others, who feel that God gave us an inquisitive brain for a reason, question the illogical premise that light was created in the universe on the first day of creation, yet the sun and stars were not created until the fourth day.

Scientifically, there is no way *physical light* could have filled the universe before the sun and stars appeared. Even after the sun and all the billions of stars were created, space continues to be mostly dark. However, if the Seven Day Creation Story is viewed as psychological truth, rather than historical fact, it helps us to remove not only the nonsensical aspects of this sacred text, but also provides us with a more relevant teaching.*

The original light was the spark of insight. It allowed us to recognize the truth of some superior idea. By superior idea, I mean any concept that challenges us to look beyond satisfying our personal appetites. Ideas like "love thy neighbor," or "ask not what your country can do for you, ask what you can do for your country." When we embrace such ideas, the light of understanding reaches into our inner garden. We begin to think differently and see things differently. Our inner gardens are growing, blossoming and even bearing fruit.

But now comes a very crucial point in the further evolution of our inner world. This step corresponds to the interval between the third and fourth stage (day) of the Seven Day Creation Story of the Bible. Without further sources of enlightenment for our daily inspiration, we can still fail in spite of our best intentions. This can best be illustrated by the ongoing trials and tribulations facing the worldly gardener.

*While it is not the scope of this book to venture much beyond gardening analogies, all the "far-fetched" ingredients in the Bible can be more rationally understood when a psychological meaning is applied to the literal words of the stories. Emanuel Swedenborg claimed that there were indeed historical characters and events in the Bible but that they were still used to represent spiritual truths. All ancient cultures used this technique. For instance, even though the Trojan Wars were a part of history, the journey in Homer's Odyssey was a spiritual one.

When I first decided to create my own organic garden I was "pumped." My initial excitement lasted from pouring over dozens of plant catalogs, all through the the drawing up of the garden layout, to finally going outdoors and getting all my seeds and small plants in the ground. But under the influence of this first ecstatic state I forgot one thing.

S_ _t happens.

We never fully anticipate all the obstacles which are sure to come our way. An expression used for this predicament is "your eyes were bigger than your stomach." This is when we take on more than we can chew. Our resolve is tested. We are left to ask ourselves, "Do I really want to go through with this?"

This is the condition I found myself in with my new garden after the flush of spring flowers had faded and the intensifying heat of summer made it more difficult to leave the comfort of my air-conditioned living-room. Weeds, such as wild lettuce, Canadian thistle, Japanese honeysuckle, goldenrod, cockspur and lamb's quarters began to take over. Japanese beetles, cabbage loopers, aphids, spider mites, asparagus beetles, tomato hornworms, squash borers, Colorado potato beetles, cutworms, armyworms and stink bugs prospered. And the weather never seemed to cooperate. It either rained too much, or not enough.

Same with the inner garden. Because no sooner do we decide how nice we want to be to people and nurture noble thoughts then some idiot in a car cuts us off on the way to work and we lose it. Another expression that comes to mind is "when you're up to your butt in alligators, it's hard to remind yourself that your original goal was to drain the swamp."

While these nasty surprises may often seem unfair, they are actually blessings in disguise. They serve as reality checks. These are the very reasons why we need more than our initial "spark" of enlightenment to get us through this next step in the development of our inner gardens.

If our resolve is not tested then our spiritual evolution is merely an intellectual exercise. Without opposition, no quality can be attached to the sphere of our activities. For *opposition alone provides the parameters of our character.* No pain, no gain. We cannot make our muscles grow unless we keep forcing them to work against *increased resistance.* Nor can we make our minds grow without increasing the difficulty of our studies. Since the evolution of our inner world depends on developing and maintaining high ethical and moral standards, those with the largest* and most productive inner gardens are those who sought to address and overcome the greatest amount of personal character flaws – the weeds and stink bugs of our psyche.

It is at this stage of our quest that we must make an important decision and ask, "Do I really want to go on with this?" This is why to get to the next step of our spiritual development we need outside help to provide a source of continuous inspiration. In sports we call these pep talks. In business they take the form of motivational seminars. In a place of worship they are called sermons.

When I found my excitement for working in the garden waning that first year, I looked for people with

---

*We instinctively acknowledge the size of an individual's inner world when we use the expression "how big of you to do that," to show gratitude towards a person's charitable nature. This is also why a selfish individual is referred to as a "small" person.

similar interests to help me out of my doldrums. I
joined the Dahlia Society; volunteered my Saturday
mornings to do work at the Missouri Botanical
Garden; attended lectures on a variety of topics,
including shade gardening, perennials, ornamental
trees, water gardening and the proper pruning
and grafting of fruit trees. I learned about what plants
were the most disease and insect resistant and how to
hybridize my own daylilies. And last but not least, I
could ask those who were much wiser than myself
how they overcame problems similar to my own. Plus,
I continued to read everything I could get my hands on.

Eventually I learned how to *prepare* myself for all
the ups and downs of gardening. For instance, by
putting down a thick layer of mulch on my garden soil
I wouldn't have to water as much in the summer heat.
The thick layer of mulch would also help to keep many
of the weeds down. In fact, when weeds did appear
through the thick mulch, the soil was made so soft
and friable that the weeds would pull out easily. As
far as the insects were concerned, if I simply planted
blocks of different garden plants, instead of single
varieties in long rows, I could frustrate them enough
to always guarantee a respectable harvest. And last but
not least, I had other gardening friends and experts as
a support system should some future and unexpected
challenge come my way.

But how do we prepare ourselves so as to not lose
interest in the upkeep of our inner gardens – especially
when things don't always go our way? How do we
develop and maintain high ideals in a world where
good guys seem to come in last, while unethical
behavior is often rewarded, and where immorality

often leads to celebrity? Here, the fourth stage of our inner development, is where our values and principles are really challenged. For support we must not only look outwards for help but *upwards* as well.

The sun, moon and stars mentioned in the fourth day (stage) of the biblical creation story represent permanent and continuous sources of inspiration and enlightenment, for both good times and to get us through our darkest hours (just as moonlight helps us to see in darkness and stars were used to help sailors navigate by night).

The sun, moon and stars are "heavenly" bodies, giving off their light from far above, just as high ideals give us something to look up to. But they represent a condition when high ideals take up a permanent position over our inner gardens. This is why I continuously study the scriptures, as well as the interpretations of various writers, and seek out the wisdom of those with superior insights to my own. I have even studied many of the world's religions, both East and West, occult and fundamentalist, ancient and modern. They have all added *light to the sky of my inner world.*

But gardeners are down to earth and like to get their hands dirty. They judge the value of a tool by what benefit or practical advantage it will give them. So you may now be questioning how having something analogous to the sun, moon and stars over our inner garden can have a practical value in the material world. For instance, how does all this help us not to lose our temper when some jerk treats us unfairly, or falsely accuses us of something?

Whereas in stage one we began to see the light of truth, having something analogous to the sun

constantly guiding us lets us do something more.
It lets us see into our inner garden so that we can be
fully aware of what is going on in there. It is not only
knowing truth, but *knowing oneself.* This gives us a
new objectivity and helps us not to become over
identified with external events. So let's pretend I am
standing in front of somebody who is yelling at me.
While I can hear the angry words and see the angry
face, something else is going on. I have the power to
look into my inner garden and notice the storm clouds
moving in. This is called having *presence of mind* or
having one's wits about him. With the power of presence
of mind, I realize that if I don't do something to disperse
the storm clouds building within, I too, will break out
in anger, and lash back at my adversary. So my spirit
looks upwards for enlightenment and sees the shining
rays of the those golden words *Love thy neighbor.*
By keeping those words before me I will have a much
better chance of finding a peaceful solution. I have
given myself an option, a choice, instead of a knee-jerk
reaction. Often, the simple act of staying calm can
defuse an explosive situation.

While the example used above may seem like an
oversimplification, the power to see what's going on in
our inner world, at all times, is crucial for us to act as
stewards of our own destiny. It demands that we be
alert in two worlds. It is a special kind of *consciousness*
that enables us to endure someone yelling at us
because *part of our attention* is being directed at our
inner world. Without this double attention it's impossible
to keep the storm clouds from rolling into our inner
world and causing us to lash back or worse. It gives
us the new freedom to *act* rather than *react.* We can't

control the weather of the physical world but we
can control the weather in our inner world!

This is the power to "turn the other cheek." It
is not passivity. It is the exercising of total control,
which comes not from knowledge, but self-knowledge.

When "we lose it" we actually lose sight of our
inner garden (what's going on inside us) and become
totally identified with some external situation. We
give into it and become cut off from any influences
that might be trying to reach us from our inner world.

I find the most effective way to prepare myself for
encounters with others is to start each day by asking
God to help give me the power to maintain my inner
peace throughout the day. Later, when some fool zips
his car into a parking spot that I'm heading towards,
I find myself less likely to overreact to the event.
Instead, it has no more effect on me than when I'm
watching a scene from some old movie. Because my
real attention is on my inner garden – a power gained
by having permanent sources of light to guide me.

A Green Thumb

A person who has lots of success in making plants
grow and thrive is said to have a "green thumb." The
thumb allows us to grasp things. In the first chapter
I made the point that grasping things is analogous to
understanding things. Therefore, a person with a green
thumb has better luck than others with growing things
because he or she *understands* what it takes to succeed.

First, you prepare the soil, amending it with nutrient-
rich compost. Then you purchase quality seeds. You

also study the cultural needs of each variety of plant. Next, you water, feed and watch over the plants all through the growing period, always on the watch for weeds and insect pests. Finally, you are able to reap the reward of your efforts at harvest time.

Understanding is also the green thumb of a spiritual gardener. Those who have it are very successful in making spiritual ideals grow and thrive in their inner gardens. Like those who possess green thumbs in the worldly garden, we first need to prepare the soil of our character by amending it with the proper humility to accept the seeds of superior spiritual ideas. Then we study the nutritive requirements of these ideas, knowing that they must be rooted in definite *organic* principles such as the Golden Rule and "Love Thy Neighbor". Next we must water these concepts through our continued seeking, study and application of new spiritual knowledge. As these concepts grow, mature and leaf out into full-blown belief systems (spiritual doctrines for living), we must always be on the watch for disruptive thoughts and emotional pests (deceit, envy, bitterness, and a host of self-indulgences) which may sneak in. Finally our efforts bear fruit.

The cultivation of our spiritual understanding (faith) will ensure every gardener of acquiring an "angelic" green thumb.

SPRING FEVER

At no time can the connection between our inner and outer worlds be more self-evident than with the arrival of spring every year. The lawns put on a shiny fresh green. Migrations of birds wing their way back from their winter homes. Butterflies emerge from crevices in the rough barks of trees and other forest hiding places.

The purple, yellow and white flower blooms of crocuses and the sweet fragrances of early spring daffodils and hyacinths inspire us to go out and enjoy the world again. Lovers hold hands once more in their walks through the park. We feel as if something has reawakened in us. Our spirits feel quickened. Because what we see all around us *is also being experienced inside us.* Spring, in its heightened glory, fills the world with flower and song, and so, too, our hearts and minds. As above, so below.

The increased activity of nature at this time of year not only comes from the hours of daylight increasing, but from the return of *vernal heat.* It is the coming warmth that brings new life to the garden each year. It is the return of warmth that causes the birds to sing, seeds to sprout and eggs to hatch.

Our inner garden needs a source of heat as well.

The full importance of a heavenly body, like the sun making its appearance to rule the skies above our inner gardens, is that in the fourth stage of spiritual development we receive an additional vivifying influence. The sun not only provides light to let us see, it gives us warmth!

Our spiritual evolution does not stop with enlightenment. What is knowledge, understanding, philosophy, or science, if each fails to lead us to LOVE, but an artificial or dead contrivance. Love brings harmony to cold mathematical qualities and gives us music.

Love is analogous to heat. It is the inner flame of love and passion that opens our minds to learn. It is the wamth of love that opens our hearts to do good deeds for others. It is love that energizes every aspect of our lives until they become burning desires. We cannot even move one little finger without some *desire* to do so.

What other source of warmth can bring life into our inner world? Allow things there to grow? Blossom? And bear fruit? But love! It is not "truth" which brings these things about, but the *love to do what is true* that brings everything to life. Love makes truth organic!

The appearance of the sun above our inner gardens represents a new influence guiding us throughout our daily activities. We go to work with more bounce in our step. We eagerly embrace new challenges. Passion returns to our lives. The wise words we've read from inspirational books or heard from gifted individuals during our lifetime take on new meaning. We are beginning to do things not because they are the "right" thing to do, but because they are a "good" thing to do. Evolution is now proceeding from our minds to our hearts.

So after we have seen the light (first day), separated higher principles from lower ones (second day), picked principles to stand for (third day), we next begin to look upwards, to the heavens above, for permanent sources of enlightenment to guide us both day and night. And finally, we are to open our hearts to the continuous inspiration of something even greater – the warmth of love (fourth day).

Our inner garden is now ready to evolve on another dimension.

New things are beginning to stir inside us.

STEP FIVE: CREEPING THINGS
AND FLYING FOWL

The world of Nature is made up of more than the mineral and plant kingdoms. A third kingdom evolves from it - the animal kingdom. And life takes on another level of activity. Instead of producing branches, leaves and flowers, organic life also can develop mouths, legs and wings! Life gains the power to move about and experience the world from a larger sphere.

Similarly, the mind is more than memory and thought. As our inner world evolves, we not only nurture and cultivate our ideas, we eventually put them into motion. Through our activities, our mind expands its operation to a larger sphere. Our ideas not only produce branches, leaves and flowers, but grow legs and wings and move about.

For instance, if I study the Ten Commandments and ponder their virtues, my knowledge of them

increases; but when I *practice* them, it all takes on
a new dimension, a new level of activity.

Physical motion corresponds to inner motion:
the kingdom of our desires, intentions, feelings and
appetites. It is our *emotional* world. We often refer to
a highly emotional performance from actors or public
speakers as producing a "very moving experience"
within us. That's why animals (and their various activities)
correspond to all the things of our emotional world.
We can be timid as a mouse, sly as a fox, brave as a lion,
capricious like a goat, gentle as a lamb, or innocent as
a dove. And no one can doubt the powerful emotional
connection children have with their stuffed animals.

This also explains why advertising writers have
had lots of success using "critters" as spokespersons
for everything from beer to breakfast cereals.

Writers of the past made use of this technique to
teach valuable lessons in life. Aesop's fables are well
known for their use of animals to portray human qualities.
The race between the "Hare and The Tortoise" demon-
strates how "slow and steady wins the race."

The story of Noah's Ark becomes much more relevant
and believable if we use all the animals of the world to
represent the full range of human emotions. It is our
emotions which always get us into trouble – the greed,
envy, revenge, vanity and anger in our lives that always
make things turn out bad. Therefore, it is our emotional
world that needs to be saved from disasters.* As I
pointed out in Chapter Two, since the blueprint for
the Ark came from God's specifications, it represented

*This is why the Lord was born in a manger where animals are kept. He is
to be born within our hearts. Otherwise, there's no room for Him in our busy
schedules (the inn in town).

His Divine doctrine or teaching. By "getting on board" we accept God's tenets to help carry our emotions over troubled water and back to the safety of dry land (character formed from spiritual principles).

This is why the animal kingdom does not emerge in the Seven Day Creation story until the fifth day, and only after the plant kingdom is established.

Just as insects, frogs, birds and other creatures find food and shelter among the protective leaves and branches of the plant world, our emotions find nourishment and protection among the various thoughts, ideas and teachings we cultivate. Our knowledge and understanding must develop first before the proper emotions can appear. A desert corresponds to an inner world with little knowledge (little water). This inner desolation creates an environment inhospitable for the character to fully develop and leaves a person without the proper tools to resist the temptations of the world. This is why "lowly" creatures, such as snakes, rodents, tarantulas and scorpions thrive in such an environment. A horse won't thrive eating cactus, nor will the desire to be nice to people be nourished by the kind of narrow thinking which convinces us of our superiority over others.

Proper thinking attracts proper actions. Therefore, our inner garden must develop through proper thinking based on the spiritual (organic) principles of reciprocal cooperation. Nature progressed by the perfection of mutual cooperation between its evolving plant and animal kingdoms. This reciprocating dynamic is known in religious jargon as *charity*. As our understanding grows, so does the scope of our activity. At first, we do simple good deeds by being civil and

respectful. Later, as we learn more, our desire grows
to do the greatest amount of good for the greatest
amount of people, such as joining groups and various
organizations to share our talents with others. Finally,
special individuals accomplish things which benefit
not only their own generation but the generations that
will follow through works of art, books and scientific
discoveries. Evolution is love increasing its sphere of
activity – both within Nature and within us!

Most gardeners observe that the greater the diversity
of plants a garden contains, the more varied the
wildlife it attracts. For twenty years I have watched
this process take place in my garden. In this way, I
have verified for myself how the evolution of life on
this planet was a perfect similitude for how each of
us can become more "alive" from within.

In 1979, I purchased five acres of Illinois farmland.
I wanted to raise my family in a more natural lifestyle.
My vision for this property was to literally try to create
a small Eden. The key here is the word "create,"
because the property I was to set my roots down in
was anything but what could be described as "the
good earth."

The land had been planted in soybeans at the time
of the purchase. That fall, even before building the
house, I decided to plant a few trees on the property
because I was anxious to start making it look like the
paradisiacal vision I had for it. My vision was to grow
the widest diversity of trees possible, since the Garden
of Eden was described as containing "every tree that is
pleasant to the sight and good for food" (Gen 2:9). So I
started with a weeping willow, Carolina silverbells,

black walnut, filbert, and apple tree. I remember having
to work harder than usual with the shovel. In fact, I
had never had such a difficult time digging a few simple
holes in my entire life. At the depth of about a foot,
the work became almost impossible as I had hit a
layer of greyish looking soil called *hardpan*. Hardpan
is a condition where the soil is compacted almost to
the point of being cement. It is caused after years of
subjecting the same soil to modern farming (chemical)
methods and heavy farm equipment. What surprised
me even more was that I hadn't uncovered a single
earthworm in all my digging!

I had wrongly assumed that farmland automatically
meant fertile soil. The soil below my feet was lifeless.
This hardpan reminds me of people who stop learning
after they leave school and unquestioningly follow the
beaten path once they enter the work force. They
resist new ideas and feel threatened by change. It is
a well known fact that children can learn new things
much easier than adults. This is because they are open
to the world and have not had time to form biases or
become set in their ways.

*"Truly, I say to you, whoever does not receive the kingdom
of God like a child shall not enter it."*
(Mk 10:15)

*"Be the stream of the universe! Being the stream of the
universe, Ever true and unswerving, Become as a little child
once more."*
(Tao Te Ching 28)

We cannot accept new ideas until we yield to
them. I find it highly significant that the term *yield*

means both "allowing" and "productivity." I suspect that many people who resist new thinking allow their inner worlds to become like farm acreage, with row after monotonous row of corn or soybeans, or mile after mile of unending wheat. While getting 220 bushels of corn from one acre may seem productive, it is not as productive as an acre of land planted in fruit trees, berries, nuts and a wide variety of vegetables and root crops. Variety is the spice of life. People who fall into a routine can get a lot done in their jobs but still feel unfulfilled if they are not *open* to new ideas or challenges. A diversity of ideas and interests is what fills in the emptiness of our inner gardens.

Monoculture above, monoculture below.

So like hardpan (compacted soil) we have to "open up" and become more yielding.

I was determined to make the hard clay soil on my property yield to my wishes. I wanted it to support a variety of plants and attract a variety of animal life, particularly song birds and butterflies. This did not happen overnight. The first couple of years after I bought my property I simply let the weeds grow. I took advantage of their toughness and ability to send roots deep into the hard soil and bring up valuable minerals to the surface. Then I would have a farmer or a lawn mowing service come in with a tractor and brush hog and mow it all down. I let the cut weeds lie where they were and naturally break down to increase the organic matter. I also planted nitrogen-fixing legumes, like clover and alfalfa, among the weed stubble. Later, topsoil, manure, and bales of straw were trucked in. I used the topsoil to fill in the holes for the next round of trees I was planting and piled up thick layers of straw around each tree as a water conserving and weed smothering mulch. The manure was mixed with additional topsoil to build up the raised beds of my vegetable garden. Finally I built two compost piles where I could dump all my garden refuse, mowed leaves and grass clippings, all to later be returned to and enrich the garden soil.

I now have a garden area of about 50'X100'. It includes not only vegetables and culinary herbs of all kinds, but a grape arbor, raspberries, blackberries, quince, currants, gooseberries, strawberries, hardy kiwi, elderberries, serviceberries, bush (pie) cherries and bamboo shoots.

I planted over three hundred fruit, nut, shade and ornamental trees throughout the entire five acres. This includes six kinds of maple, seven kinds of oak, plus a variety of pine trees, spruce, cypress, juniper, larch, beech, magnolia, apples, pears (including oriental pears), cherries, peaches, apricot, mulberries, persimmons, pawpaw, pecan, hickory, filbert, black walnut, English walnut, and chestnuts.

Finally the day came when I could put my shovel into the ground and lift out a clump of dirt containing living, squirming worms – hallelujah!

Over the years, as my trees and plantings matured, I succeeded in attracting a virtual zoo of animals onto my property. Garden toads, tree frogs, leopard frogs, bull frogs, spotted salamanders,* box turtles, painted turtles, snapping turtles, skinks (a small lizard), crawfish, garter and black snakes, shrews, moles, squirrels,

---

*I am particularly proud of the amphibians I have attracted to my garden since their numbers are declining throughout the world. They also eat slugs and other garden pests!

ground hogs, rabbits, grey and red fox, coyote, raccoon, muskrats, possum and deer.

Every now and then some of these "critters" cause a problem to the garden and fruit trees, but generally they all seem to keep each other in check. I have made no sightings of skunk yet, which I attribute to the fact that there is a mating pair of Great Horned Owls nesting in the adjoining woods each year.

Speaking of birds, the diversity of trees, shrubs and other plant life in my garden helped to attract the kinds of feathered wonders that could only be found in a field guide: indigo buntings, bobwhite quail, warblers, herons, egrets, falcons, hummingbirds, orioles, goldfinches, grosbeaks, cedar waxwings, tufted titmice, kingfishers, and bluebirds.

Among the flowers and shrubs I have also enjoyed the monarch butterfly, tiger swallowtail, black swallowtail, giant swallowtail, zebra swallowtail, red admiral, gray hairstreak, sulfer, morning cloak, skippers, coppers, blues, painted lady, question mark, frillitaries and buckeyes.

I am not suggesting that everyone has to do all this for spiritual growth, or even to garden for that matter, but it provides a beautiful picture of how our inner garden becomes more energized and animated when we strive to keep challenging ourselves to learn new things and cultivate new interests. Anybody can become an inner gardener!

WATER GARDENS AND PONDS

As gardeners increase the diversity of growing things in their gardens they can become inspired to create additional interest to the landscape – water gardens and small ponds. Or, if they are lucky enough to have a natural pond near their garden, they might plant water-loving plants along its shore and water lilies within the actual water. Taking water gardening even further, they can add fountains, waterfalls and colorful fish, like gold-fish or Japanese koi.

Likewise, new dimensions of mental activity are added to our inner gardens. We can now create psychological water gardens and ponds. And as our inner world evolves, everything is affected. For instance, when we cultivate a diversity of thoughts and interests it also has a reciprocal effect on our memory. Water represents knowledge, and bodies of water (collections of knowledge) in our inner garden represent our memory. Adding fountains and fish to a pond reflect the dynamic psychological changes taking place in our memory. Fountains represent knowledge put into motion or *knowledge that is useful and relevant to our lives.* This is why living fish can now enter the scene. The things in our memory are no longer just a static collection of various data. The data can now be organized and arranged into more dynamic and animated forms – like fish. This is what happens when the things we memorize become classified into various species of ideas that we find most interesting. For instance, if within my memory I find scientific data the most interesting, I will arrange that information into enjoyable patterns. Fish can have interesting and colorful patterns because they represent how we pattern our knowledge into the form most interesting to us. In this way our memory becomes more vivified. We call this more active memory our *imagination.*

*And God created great whales, and every living thing that
creepeth, which the waters made to creep forth, after their kinds,
and every winged foul after its kind; and God saw that it
was good.*
                                        (Gen 1:21)

The Bird Feeder

Bird feeders are another way to attract birds into
the garden besides having a diversity of trees, shrubs
and flowers. Spiritually, birds represent our higher
aspirations because they have the power of flight, just
as the human mind does when it takes the higher or
wider view of things. Beautiful birds abound in an
inner garden where the gardener finds beauty in the
greater objectivity of spiritual ideas.

Having a birdfeeder in our inner garden is like a
person who is prepared to provide higher aspirations
(noble thoughts of helping our neighbor) with sustaining
food. Seeds make up the bulk of the food found in the
bird feeder. Everytime we *intend* or *will* something, we
create psychological seeds (like the germ of an idea).
Seeds represent ideas distilled from our memory and
concentrated into a form to promote some purpose. The
more useful our ideas, the more they can become the
food for our higher, spiritual aspirations. Objectivity
needs a noble purpose to sustain itself and keep it
aloft.

Garden Pests

Garden pests are any kind of creatures whose activities
threaten the productivity of the garden. Similarly, the

pests which attack our inner garden are the pesky emotions and feelings which can often plague us. Anger, jealousy, pettiness, one-upsmanship, and revenge can all devour and destroy the fruits of our labors overnight, leaving stubble where thoughts of kindness once flourished.

Nowhere in the physical world do pests like Colorado potato beetles, corn borers, and locusts get out of control than in areas where monoculture is practiced. In Nature, everything is kept in check and balance by the diversity of life. The more varied the plant life in an area, the more varied the animal life. This increases the chances that unwanted pests will fall prey to other creatures.

In our inner garden the same dynamics apply. Those who cultivate a diversity of thoughts and who constantly seek to get a higher and more objective view of the world can create an inner environment that is more emotionally balanced and keep destructive emotions in-check.

BUTTERFLIES

Not all caterpillars turn out bad. Since they crawl around and gorge themselves in our garden all day they represent our primitive appetites for self-gratification. Similarly, once our inner garden becomes more balanced and we recognize the destructive powers of total self-gratification, we can strive for a more refined food. Like the caterpillar that goes through metamorphosis and changes into a winged butterfly, our desires can rise above the corporeal sphere and reach up for spiritual knowledge, which is like the sweet nectar distilled in flowers.

THE FOOD CHAIN

Just as the outer world is arranged in a graded series of life forms which feed off each other, so too does our inner world. Everyday our inner world becomes a jungle of thoughts and emotions fighting for survival or dominion. Unlike Nature, which allows only the fittest to survive, man alone determines what thoughts and feelings are to rule his inner world. We can see how this drama is played out within our minds by providing the correct psychological equivalents to the creatures which take part in Nature's food chain.

An eagle is keen-sighted and can soar thousands of feet above the ground and therefore represents the highest level of our rationality and foresight.* Symbolically, when an eagle swoops down to catch a fish, it represents our rationality coming down to feed from the things swimming around in our memory (water); you cannot be rational unless you can draw upon ideas and experiences from the memory – after having first discerned them from a higher vantage point.

On the other hand, it would be against the true order of things if a shark could jump out of the water to snap up a low flying eagle. Symbolically, this would represent a more deadly and dangerous side of our imagination coming up to destroy our rationality. This is what we do when we conspire to do harm to others. Ruthless people are often called "sharks."

---

*I find it ironic that the bald eagle suffered greatly from the use of the now banned pesticide DDT – artificial solutions often display man's limited scope and lack of foresight.

The Bible makes use of similar imagery in the story of Jonah being swallowed by a whale. This famous story warns us of the dangers to our inner life if we get swallowed up by huge generalities (i.e., fat people are lazy, women can't drive, and all men are helpless) which can dwell in our memory and keep us in spiritual vagueness. So, according to the food chain we establish in our inner world, evil can make its appearance.

The best definition I've ever heard for describing evil is that it is the *reversal of order.* In nature, the higher forms of life live off the lower forms of life. Toads eat bugs and worms, snakes eat toads, birds of prey and mammals eat snakes, and at the top of the food chain is man. When man is attacked by insects, snakes, sharks or lions, they are not only seen as evil creatures but symbolize lower forms of intelligence getting the upper hand on higher forms of intelligence. This reversal of order in the food chain is the main dynamic behind most horror movies depicting everything from werewolves and vampire bats to amoeba-type blobs. It is as if we all instinctively sense some deeper terror in these movies that transcends the physical harm such *inferior* creatures would inflict.

Legends of monsters, serpents and dragons represented lower forms of life which gained dominion of a man's inner world. To turn into a werewolf is to allow our hearts to become more cunning and deceptive (a wolf in sheep's clothing). The serpent in the Garden of Eden was forced to crawl on its belly because it symbolized mankind's total immersion into (from head to toe) and preference for "worldly" things, and the earthly delights of his corporeal and sensual nature. This is the *reversal of order* within mankind's inner world – when rationality and intelligence are overthrown by the cupidities of our five senses, which are

represented by lower forms of life. It is not that we are
to rid our inner garden of snakes and reptiles, they
have their place and serve a sacred purpose just as our
five corporeal senses serve the higher mind. It's that the
mind should not be in servitude to our lowest nature.

We "listen" to the serpent of our inner world when
we reject the highest or widest view in preference for
the lowest and most subjective point of view. This is
why correcting this state is symbolized by the Caduceus*
in Greek mythology: a pair of snakes weaving up a staff
with wings at the top. This emblem represents turning
our lower nature upwards (getting the snake off its
belly) towards spiritual ideals (wings).

Mankind's misjudgements and blunders are all rooted
in self-guidance. We all know what happens to a society
when people all choose to go their own way, when
athletes on the same team all seek to be the superstar,
or when as citizens we choose to bypass the laws of
state and country. The power to organize and maintain
order always comes from "above." A road crew working
on a new highway would not know where to go unless
they were guided by a map representing a *higher
vantage point.* The stomach, liver, heart and lungs
would be of no value to the body if their activities
were not orchestrated. Cancer is cellular anarchy.

The true wisdom of nature is in her ability to
restore, maintain and promote the true order of
things. This is called harmony.

The true purpose of all religion is to restore balance
and order to our inner ecosystem – to bring us back to
the garden of spiritual harmony. It warns us that it can
only come from a higher vantage point.

God's will be done, not our will.

---

*Few medical doctors are aware that the symbol for their own profession
has its roots in spiritual healing.

THE WORLD OF NATURE AND THE NATURE OF MAN

The deeper we go with our analogy between our outer world and our inner world, the more profound will be the promise of things that are uncovered.

Let's now look even deeper into the wonderful workings of Nature and see what more she can teach us about inner growth, harmony and order.

When tender plants emerge from the soil each spring, their leaves rise to meet the sun, while roots penetrate into the soil. The purpose of leaves is to collect sunlight and gases, such as carbon dioxide from the atmosphere, while roots bring up water and elements like calcium, boron, iron, zinc, and magnesium from the soil below. Plants combine this atmospheric and earthly material into new *biomass*. In other words – growth.

Now let's see if something similar happens psychologically.

When I attempt to look inward, it becomes self-evident that all my thoughts are rooted in the various things of my memory (water in the soil) which have relation to my convictions (soluble minerals). As I bring these ideas up from my memory, new information is constantly coming into my senses (leaves) from the outside world (air and sun).

Everyday the mind is constantly mixing our old convictions with new ideas, old experiences with new ones. Then it reorganizes this material to produce new *psychomass*, or intellectual growth.

When plant leaves have served their purpose and become old, they wither and fall to the ground. As they break down through the action of acids in the soil, and by the digestive systems of earthworms and other soil microbes, their constituent parts are returned to the soil. However, something even more dynamic is taking place than conservation. The soil not only gets all its original material back, but it also gets all the new material absorbed and created by the the leaf from the atmosphere and the sun, such as sugars and starches! So, more is put back than was taken out, not to mention that everything is returned back to the soil in a more *exalted* form.

The same is true with our inner world.

Once our thoughts and mental constructions have served their purpose, they fade and fall back into the soil of our convictions. But since this intellectual material was also formed by the addition of new information coming from the outer world, as it withers and is broken down to its component parts, the principles we stand for (the ground of our beliefs) are continually added to, perfected and perpetually refined.

In Nature, as soil becomes more fertile, it becomes suitable for larger and more complex plants to emerge, plants whose roots go deeper into the soil and whose superior leaves reach higher into the sky. This expanding environment attracts insects, amphibians and birds, whose activities pollinate flowers, fertilize the soil, and spread seeds even further through their droppings. As plants and animals both evolve, *new connections* and *relationships* are perfected. A food chain is established to ensure the balance and maintain the order of the ecosystem.

Likewise, as our mind becomes more fertile our intellect grows and evolves into more highly organized ideas. Understanding and thought are the ability to draw out and find *new connections* between things, to discover *new relationships.* The more coherent we become, the more we can increase and widen the sphere of our activities. And it all proceeds by organic processes that are totally analogous with nature.

Just as the mineral kingdom is exalted and rises to the level of plants and animals through the course of evolution, our inner evolution causes our principles to rise up through our thoughts and then through our actions. Our inner world becomes organized into a *hierarchy of values.*

This is why a garden symbolizes wisdom.

The arrangement of everyone's inner world is of course different, since people have different values. *What we love most takes the highest position* within our inner garden. If we prefer worldly rewards over spiritual rewards, however, our inner life will correspond to a world that is dominated and ruled by lower forms of life.

TRUE ORDER	THE REVERSAL OF ORDER
1) Love of God	1) Love of the world
2) Love of all humanity	2) Love of riches
3) Love of the neighbor	3) Love of power
4) Civility	4) Civility
5) Love of power	5) Love of the neighbor
6) Love of riches	6) Love of all humanity
7) Love of the world	7) Love of God

The fall of "Man" is the reversal of order and his removal from wisdom. It is interesting to note that this reversal of values may have even subconsciously entered into our daily language when we refer to the bottom of the foot as our *sole.**

For those of my readers who will demand to know why the above lists are not arbitrary, let me now explain why this value system cannot be otherwise. First, love of the world is corporeal. It is the lowest of all values because it involves bodily pleasure and creature comforts. The love of riches is superior to sensory and corporeal pleasures because it involves the imagination. It recognizes bodily pleasure as inferior because it will sacrifice this pleasure to accumulate wealth. Above this is the love of power, or self love. This involves more of our intellectual side which seeks fame, celebrity, notoriety, and political clout, and will gladly spend all its riches and wealth to achieve it. Next is civility. People have to be able to sacrifice their love to have power over others in order to treat them equally and with true respect. This ideal is superior to the love of gaining power because it prefers rationality over cunning. Love of the neighbor is higher yet. Here we become spiritually rational. Our sense of duty moves from the mind to the heart. Love of all humanity is superior yet because it includes people of all races, nationalities, and religions. Love of God represents the highest and most objective expression of neighborly love since it embraces all things.

---

*I admit this is no more than a hunch. However, the word sole is derived from the Latin word for sandal (solea), which is derived from the Latin word for base (solum). Certainly, anyone who embraces "worldly principles" has his soul oriented to the earth – an upside-down man!

This order – of expanding the sphere of love – is also observed in the Tao Te Ching (54):

> *Cultivate Virtue in your self,*
> *And Virtue will be real.*
> *Cultivate it in the family,*
> *And Virtue will abound.*
> *Cultivate it in the village,*
> *And Virtue will grow.*
> *Cultivate it in the nation,*
> *And Virtue will be abundant.*
> *Cultivate it in the universe,*
> *And Virtue will be everywhere.*

Our inner garden (wisdom) evolves up through this evolutionary ladder or hierarchy of values. But none of this can happen until we become more yielding. The ground has to yield to the seed. Minerals in the soil must be broken down by acids to release their potentials. Even a seed must break out of its hard covering, by yielding to the enlivening forces of spring rain and the sun's warmth, before it can become a new plant. The phoenix can only rise after it has fallen into ashes. A butterfly cannot emerge without first sacrificing the caterpillar. Winter must come to the world before spring can return. For new scientific theories to prevail, old theories must fall to the wayside. Our love for power has to yield to a love for the neighbor. Death brings new life.

TWO WORLDS, TWO DEATHS

Spiritual growth begins when we submit to a higher power. Within our inner garden, it is the death of old beliefs, either about ourselves, or the world we live in, that allows new influences to take hold. Old ideas die hard. In fact, you could say that life is one great big death struggle between self-centeredness and love towards others. Spiritual growth requires that something of our inner world must pass away even before the death of our physical body. This is exactly the "death" that the Lord talked about in the Bible.

"He who conquers shall not be hurt by the second death."
(Rev 2:11)

"Blessed and holy is he who shares in the first resurrection! Over such the second death has no power..."
(Rev 20:6)

Other biblical passages allude to this as well:

"Truly, truly, I say to you, unless a grain of wheat falls to the earth and dies, it remains alone; but if it dies, it bears much fruit. He who loves his life loses it, and he who hates his life in this world will keep it for eternal life."
(John 12:24,25)

"Truly, truly, I say to you, unless one is born anew, he cannot see the kingdom of God."
(John 2:3)

"But I tell you truly, there are some standing here who will not taste death before they see the kingdom of God."
(Lk 9:27)

Muhammed used these words:

"Die before you are dead."

And from the eighteenth century esoteric Islamic teacher, Shaikh Ahmad Ahsa'i's meditations on the "diamond body":

"Every individual rises again in the very form which his Work* has fixed in the secret depth of himself."

In my own life there are many old habits which I wish were "dead and gone," ideas and impulses that I would like to "lay to rest," but which I am still struggling with. In each case my self-pride still gets in the way. These are thoughts and feelings that I have as yet spared from the compost heap. Humility, like the humus created from the *dead* and *decaying* waste of the compost pile, sets the whole process of spiritual growth in progress. And keeps it going!

COMPOST - THE MORE THE BETTER

Simply stated, the compost pile is merely an apparatus for concentrating (and speeding up) the forces of Mother Nature. Therefore, within the workings of the compost pile, we shall also discover a similar mechanism for speeding up the actions that spiritual forces can have on our lives. In other words, each of us can progress and evolve as fast as we are *willing* to!

Whereas the compost pile of the worldly garden quickens or speeds up the production of *humus*, the inner compost pile, as alluded to earlier, hastened the development of *humility*.

*I interperet the word "work" in this context to mean Spiritual Struggle.

Illness, personal loss and the feebleness of old age can certainly help us to find humility, but are circumstances mostly out of our control. In the inner compost pile, *reflection, self-examination* and *introspection* takes the place of turning over old leaves and garden refuse with the pitchfork. Are we as nice as we think we are, as smart as we think we are, or as important as we think we are? This activity makes the work of inner growth proceed much faster because we have full control over the repetition and intensity of such scrutiny.

But old leaves are not turned into humus without heat, just as old ideas and habits are not turned into humility without *remorse* (spiritual smoldering). Remorse is more than self-examination. It includes *confession*, the admission of finding a character flaw, and *repentance*, the resolve to change. This is what allows higher forces (spiritual lessons) to break down any unflattering aspects of our inner world and begin reconstituting it more favorably towards some greater good.

The more we expose and submit ourselves to this humbling process *the faster our evolution proceeds.* This process cannot take place in people who are stubborn and who hold on to their vanity, prejudices and who insist on the fulfillment of every little self-satisfying aim. Just as a compost pile cannot break down actively living plant material, our inner compost pile cannot break down ideas we keep alive. We must acknowledge and allow ourselves to come under the influence of superior principles, principles that challenge our love to work in an ever larger sphere.

Submission is not seen here as aimlessness or a weakness, but as cooperation with something we perceive as being superior to our self-centered nature. This is why all those who will accept the Lord at His Second Coming will be "adorned as a bride."

"I saw the holy city, new Jerusalem, coming down out of heaven from God, prepared as a bride for her husband."
(Rev 21:2)

Symbolically, this means, all those (men and women) who are willing to receive spiritual life.

"Now I am Your disciple, and a soul surrendered unto you. Please instruct me."
(Bhagavad-gita : Text 7)

Unfortunately, while Nature naturally evolves towards greater harmony, this does not always occur with the inner nature of man. "Humanness" has to be learned, and more importantly, chosen. This is because we cannot *appropriate* anything into our lives or make it our "property" unless we *will* it – and go after it.

Nature cannot act otherwise than it is "programmed to do." But mankind can act anyway it chooses – and does! This is God's gift to mankind, to give us the freedom to create our own inner garden ... or inner desert, to adopt certain principles and reject others.

"For where your treasure is, there will your heart be also."
(Lk 12:34)

Of all the creatures in the world, this is why we are given the longest period of time for our brains to develop and learn before we go out into the world.

The evolution of Homo sapiens was not so much
that he learned to stand upright, as his learning to
stand upright on spiritual principles. It was not so
much the discovery of fire, for light and warmth, as
it was the discovery of God, for *enlightenment* and
the *warmth of spiritual love.* Men and women evolved
out of nature so that an inner world could evolve out
of them!

Evolution can neither be scientifically understood,
nor can the Bible be theologically understood, unless
another, more "invisible" world history is taken into
account: That man's true story takes place on another
plane.

Who cannot see that a man or woman who desires
to work with others, for the common benefit of others,
is coming from no ordinary place, but another place?

Some "higher" place.

Who cannot see that this "other place" from
which great individuals come from is not Mars,
Jupiter or Timbuctu, but from an inner garden?

STEP SIX: BRING FORTH THE LIVING SOUL

When I envision Adam and Eve strolling through paradise, enjoying fruits, nuts and berries of every kind, I see them also living in harmony among even the larger wild animals and beasts of the animal kingdom, like zebras, elephants and giraffes.

Once a garden is fairly established, larger animals begin to make their appearance. While I obviously do not have zebras, elephants or giraffes roaming about my five acres, rabbits, deer, fox, raccoons and other animals make their appearance – animals of greater complexity when compared to worms, amphibians and reptiles (creeping things). That's because as my garden matured and continued to evolve over the years, an environment was created capable of supporting higher forms of life. The more than three hundred trees I planted matured at different heights, producing tall, medium, and low canopies. The diversity of trees, shrubs, flowers and garden crops provided not only shelter for larger animals but a wide variety of food sources such as leaf crops, roots, melons, bramble berries, fruit and nut crops. Critter heaven!

The same is true with our inner garden. As our thoughts and ideas mature, blossom and bear more fruit, we create an inner ecosystem capable of supporting more highly developed (more noble) emotions and actions. For instance, the more we study science, music, art, or any other subject, the more our abilities will grow, as well as the desire to put that knowledge into practice. Similarly, the more we learn and understand that our true purpose in life is to be of service to others, the more our actions will be directed towards those aims. But one might point out that we can't make a living unless we provide some product or service to others anyway. I will just say that being of service to others simply to put food on the table merely addresses one world. Being of service to improve the lives and happiness of others means one is gainfully employed in both worlds – inner and outer. There is no other way our actions can become more noble unless they address both worlds. Besides, we tend not to work harder than we have to if our labors are restricted to one world (as opposed to increasing the sphere of those we can benefit). It's not what we do, but how and why we do it.

In the previous step of our spiritual evolution, which corresponds to the fifth day in Genesis, we attracted creeping things, fish and birds into our garden.

"And God said, Let the waters cause to creep forth the creeping thing, the living soul; and let foul fly above the earth upon the faces of the expanse of the heavens."

(Gen 1:20)

On the sixth day we attract "wild animals" and "beasts" into our inner ecosystem.

"And God said, Let the earth bring forth the living soul after its kind, the beast, and the moving thing, and the wild animal of the earth after its kind; and it was so."
(Gen 1:24)

What is most significant here about the changes now taking place within us is that our inner garden is becoming more dominated by something analogous to *warm-blooded* mammals. Remember, that since Day Four of our spiritual evolution, our inner gardens not only came under the influence of the sun's light, but also its warmth. We began to do things not only because they were right (Truth), but also because they were good (Love). The growing influence of love's warmth is represented by the emergence of larger, warm-blooded mammals into our inner garden. It signifies that our heart has now evolved equally with our mind. In modern parlance this is referred to as increasing our emotional I.Q.

The best way I can express the nature of this change is that we no longer work from just a sense of duty, but from a labor of love. Sometimes when I go out into the garden to pull the weeds or water the vegetables, I perform the tasks because I *know* I *should*. The voice of my conscience comes through loud and clear that I must accomplish these weekly garden tasks or things will get out of control.

It is altogether different when we reach the next stage of our inner evolution. It is a stage where I no longer have to dread my duties because my efforts begin to well up from the heart. I become inspired to jump into my garden tasks despite the fact that it is 90 degrees outside. What was once dreaded becomes a delight. This stage can best be summed up by the phrase *whistling while you work*. We become involved in our work, *heart* and *mind*.

BALANCE

The balance of nature is preserved through the mutual relationships of all its life-forms. The interdependence between the plant and animal kingdoms is called the ecosystem. The health of our inner ecosystem also depends upon the reciprocation between our thoughts and feelings. When our thoughts or feelings get out of whack it usually results in some kind of psychological imbalance. *Hypocrisy* is the development of the intellect (knowing what is right) without regard to the actions of the heart (doing what is wrong). *Infatuation* is an example of our emotional world manifesting without the support of judgement. Neurosis comes from the fact that the modern world teaches us very little about the upkeep and balance of our inner world.

Humanness is the proper development of, and the proper relationship between, our heart and mind.* When our words support our actions and our actions support our words there is a "marriage" between our *understanding* and *will*. This represents the appearance of a man and woman into the Garden of Eden.

---

*In the Egyptian Book of The Dead, a hieroglyph depicts a scale which weighs the deceased's heart against a bird's feather (higher ideals).

And God created man in his own image, in the image of
God created He him. Male and female created He them.
                                              (Gen 1:27)

The appearance of man and woman at this sixth
stage indicates that God has finished His work of
making us truly human from within. Being formed
in God's image does not mean to be the possessors of
two eyes, a nose, ten toes and fingers, or an upright
stance. It means that we now *think* spiritually from
our understanding, and *act* spiritually from our will.
Fairness, compassion, ethics, and morality, gain
dominion over all our worldly activities.

And God blessed them, and God said unto them, "Be fruitful,
and multiply, and replenish the earth, and subdue it; and
have dominion over the fish of the sea, and over the fowl of
the heavens, and over every living thing that creepeth upon
the earth."   *(Gen 1:28)*

Today, mankind has succeeded in subduing the
earth and gaining dominion of all its creatures to the
point of ravaging the planet and all its resources.
Yet this has not added one measure to our spiritual
growth. Therefore, God's command makes no sense
when taken at face value that He would ever confer
happiness to mankind by such destruction of the
environment. It makes total sense, however, that our
spiritual understanding (man) and will (woman) ought
to subdue our inner world and have dominion over
all our thoughts and feelings.

This also explains why Adam and Eve could walk
around the garden without any fear from the wild

animals and beasts. It represents a state within our
inner garden where we have mastered all our emotions.
For instance, if we overcome the temptation to deceive
people, the wolves within our inner garden will not
bother us. If we abandon cruelty and treachery of any
kind we will be able to live in peace with the tigers
and leopards which may be lurking within. Certainly,
"The wolf shall dwell with the lamb" (Is 11:6) refers
to such a reconciliation.

From all this I hope my readers will now see that
it was not a "woman" who was responsible for the fall
of man. It is our *will* that is first tempted within our
inner garden. Then our will (Eve) turns to our understanding (Adam) to rationalize our choices. This is
exactly what happens when we *desire* a big piece of
black forest chocolate cake and *rationalize* that one
little piece won't hurt – even after deciding to go
on a diet.

But certainly an apple or any other kind of fruit
is much better for us than chocolate cake. So what
makes fruit something forbidden? How can taking a
bite out of a nutritious piece of fruit not only damn
the partaker, but damn the rest of humanity down
through history? Some people believe it was a mere
act of disobedience – when God commands you not to
do something, you simply don't do it. But nowhere in
the Ten Commandments of the Bible does it ever say
"Thou shalt not eat of a certain fruit." However, the
Bible does state that the *fruit of one's labors* can be
judged!

When Adam and Eve ate this particular fruit, it
symbolized our *understanding* and *will* favoring its own

prudence over God's – "Ye shall be as gods." (Gen 3:5). *Eating* symbolizes taking some notion and "swallowing it whole." (It is not uncommon that we refer to unsavory characters as bad apples.)

Up to this point, God has called each progressive step in the evolution of our inner garden as "good." But at the end of our sixth stage, where *understanding* and *love* rule our inner world together, like partners in a marriage, it is now seen as "very good."

"And God saw everything that He had made, and behold it was very good."

(Gen 1:31)

STEP SEVEN: REST! REST?

We've reached Nirvana! Cosmic consciousness! Transcendental peace! A state of bliss! This is the true Promised Land – the development of our *inner* real estate into a paradisiacal garden. Heaven (eternal happiness) is not some place you go or have to wait for when you die. It is something you become from within.

The Creator's work is now done. He has created us anew and given us a place that no one can take from us. For it is the light of God's truth and the warmth of God's love that we have chosen to be the life-giving sun over our inner garden.

But are we to rest? I hope not.

There are too many beautiful things going on in this paradisiacal garden for snoozing in the old hammock or rocking chair. After all, we can now feel young again. Our inner world is at the height of spring. Paradise is not a place you seek for one's spiritual retirement. It is full of wonderful activity. Our inner garden is teeming with life – the spiritual principles we've chosen to live by have grown and branched out into every conceivable thought that can benefit others. These unselfish thoughts blossom into a celebration of joy, like flowers heralding the coming of good things in the form of bells, trumpets, fireworks, and rays of the sun. The ideas in our memory have come alive and begin to swim around like the most beautiful of tropical fish to produce a more vivid imagination. Our reasoning powers gain the power of flight and rise aloft as we take an ever more objective and higher view of things. The warmth of kindness emanates from all our actions. In fact, it is all this spontaneous and harmonious *activity* which gives our Paradise its beauty.

So what rest awaits us all at this seventh and last stage?

The difference is we have now reached such a state of inner balance and wholeness, that we no longer have to struggle from inner conflict. The weeds and pests are gone. Our inner worries and insecurities are all *put to rest.* We "yield" to a higher power.

"O scion of Bharata, surrender unto Him utterly. By his grace you will attain transcendental peace and the supreme and eternal abode."

(Bhagavad-gita : Text 62)

"Goodness" and "rightness" no longer have to be intellectually weighed or debated. Not even one thought now stands between the desire and the action. Everything is spontaneous. And unconditional. Goodness and rightness have now become our nature.

One simply loves to LOVE!

Everyone has experienced to some degree, even on this earthly plane, what heaven is like. We know what it feels like when everything is going right. We become both deeply involved in our work yet strangely separated from it, as though something in us has finally learned to get out of the way. I remember when I was the top scorer in my first high school basketball game. I had unselfishly carried out all the things that the coach had asked of me. But when I went home that night my performance got the best of me, and I attempted to predict how many points I would score over the first full season. Then I proceeded to conjecture how many points I could amass during my junior and senior years, and assured myself that I would break the school scoring record.

Within three weeks I found myself sitting on the bench.

True success is a magical state in which our energies flow freely to meet the task at hand. It is not the absence of work or the absence of a worthy challenge, but the perfecting of our God-given abilities to unselfishly meet these challenges. The reward is in our capacity to take on more challenges.

Living is *doing*, not getting. And Heaven is a job well done!

This is when we feel at one with the world, at peace with the world. And more importantly, at peace with ourselves. Because our daily duties are accomplished without any turmoil, scandal or hidden agendas, we are happy to cooperate.

Why?

Because it is our inner garden which has gained dominion over and reshaped our outer world. In other words, it isn't what the world brings our way that determines our happiness, but how we react to it, which is always reflected by what's going on *inside* us – what we've allowed to grow and take hold in our inner world. That is why the Promised Land cannot be otherwise than the happiness and peace gained from within.

Again, the world of Nature is perfectly analogous to human nature, or world of our spirit. As above, so below. Therefore, the simple backyard garden of peas, cabbage, tomatoes, earthworms, toads and birds literally holds the deepest secrets of life...the meaning of it all. It reveals to us God's true plan for us.

The more we observe how the backyard garden evolves, the more the true nature of Nirvana and Heavenly Bliss is revealed to us. We witness how the soil, plants and animals exalt each other through their interconnectedness and reciprocation. For here, we discover *the perfection of unity through diversity*!

Each living plant and animal adds to the perfection of the world around it. Within nature's ecosystem (and its reciprocation) the true nature and intent of its Creator becomes visible to us. But what is this Great Divine Plan that a simple garden can now make apparent to us?

What invisible inner force best represents Nature's perfection of unity through diversity? What dynamic could be responsible for the evolution of Nature's complex relationships and their reciprocation to form a most grand and harmonious ecosystem?

I can only say that for me it is the same invisible force that brings about the evolution and harmony of my inner garden.

LOVE!

Isn't LOVE the sharing of what is one's own with others? Doesn't love increase as men and women interrelate and reciprocate for the benefit of all? Doesn't love towards others lift us above our pettiness, narrowness and faults? I know I am a completely different person when I am giving to others as opposed to just taking.

There is no other force in the world with the power to arrange and organize itself into living systems for the purpose of providing some valuable function, some extra benefit, than love. Each organ in our body provides some valuable function for the purpose of benefiting *all the other organs.* Only love has the big picture in mind. Only love has providence. There is no other power which causes men to come together and organize their different talents than the desire to accomplish some greater use.

Organic means *living organization.* The more organized life is, the more ability it has to provide higher and more complex functions. The stomach digests food while the brain digests ideas. The higher the function, the more "life" it enjoys. Life can only arise out of and organize itself according to some purpose.

Therefore, the evolution of the world cannot be looked at as a serendipity of cosmic accidents. Nor can the evolution of increasingly more intelligent LIFE be looked at as the result of the "survival of the fittest," or "natural selection," which are the outcome of a totally materialistic observation of nature. Evolution is a *spiritual force* working through nature. And finally it becomes *conscious* in the inner nature of men and women.

It is the exaltation of LOVE, the perfection of Love! And it reaches its highest expression in mankind. This is why God has given mankind an inner world, so that love can become psycho-active, that is, *willed.*

In the beginning God made heaven and earth. In other words, HE created two worlds – an inside and outside. In this way, God's *Circle of Love* descends through the evolution, renewal and healing of nature's ecosystem and can return back (organically) through the perfection of our inner ecosystem!

We are not only the stewards of the earth, but we are also the stewards of our inner ecosystem. Genesis is the *generating* of an inner garden.

The Kingdom of Heaven is *within* us. That is why the Christian Scriptures stress we should clean the inside of the cup.

"Thou blind Pharisee, cleanse first that which is within the cup and platter, that the outside of them may be clean also."
(Matt 23:26)

There is no other way to find paradise. No other place to look for it. For the Lord has already appeared to men on earth – and rather than change the world through Divine force, He only asked that *we change.*

"My kingship is not of this world..."
(John 18:36)

If God's kingship is not of this world, then why should we expect the Lord's triumphant return to the physical world to cast out all evil and remove all the injustices of the outer world? Can there be any more suitable place for the Lord's return than one's inner garden? Shouldn't the Second Coming be a Divine appearance in your *second* or *inner* garden, on soil built of heavenly principles for living (God's true kingship)?

Doesn't mankind first see the Lord with their eyes (first coming), and only later do they finally see the Lord with their understanding (second coming)? Isn't Revelation an enlightening? And when we are enlightened doesn't God appear through the clouds and notions that have obscured our minds?

"Behold he cometh with clouds, and every eye shall see him...
(Rev 1:7)

While the idea of the Second Coming occurring within us might seem foreign at first, the Lord Himself said the event would not be *physically* witnessed.

"The kingdom of God cometh not with observation: neither shall they say, Look here! or, look there! For, behold, the kingdom of God is within you."
(Luke 17:20-21)

I can't imagine the Lord making "all things new" in a more meaningful way than when a man or woman gains a peaceful inner garden. Nor can I imagine how we can claim to be reborn without being active spiritual gardeners. Most of all, I cannot fathom how the Lord, after 2000 years, could still keep the promise to return within *one generation*, unless it were within *one's inner Genesis*.

"Truly, I say to you, this generation will not pass away till all this has taken place."
(Luke 21:32)

As I contemplate the "Second Coming" for myself, it becomes obvious that no matter how many perceived enemies I were to defeat, or competitors I were to outwit, my inner world would not progress one tiny step. How I'm treated by the outside world has no real effect on my inner world.

Real change goes much deeper than that. And so must the real conflict. If God were to destroy all my worldly enemies, and everyone else who I thought ought to be "wiped out," I *would still have myself to face.*

THE VICTORY GARDEN

When I was growing up as a kid in the 1950s there were still several victory gardens surrounded by pretty white picket fences in the neighborhood. These gardens were called victory gardens because if you grew your own food you were helping the war effort by not being a drain on the country's food supply.

But a better definition of a true victory garden is when we as spiritual gardeners help in the war effort against our true inner enemies, not from the invasions by foreign countries but the invasions from influences foreign to living spiritually. The inner gardener who decides to create a real victory garden is not afraid to go up against and weed out his personal biases and character flaws.

Do not the forces of good and evil find their true battleground within each of us? Are we not put in a daily situation of fighting with our personal demons, of choosing between right and wrong, or taking the high road over the lower road?

Can the Beast of the Apocalypse wage war successfully any place other than from within?

Do we not experience earthquakes when we suddenly see the "light" and must give up wrongly held views? Or feel shaken when we detect our own shortcomings? Does it not feel like the end of the world is upon us when we make the awful discovery that the enemy is us? But remember, this becomes the material that breaks down and becomes the humus of our inner compost pile. If we are not afraid to find true humility, a miraculous process can begin to create a most breathtaking world from within – filling an inner void with beautiful vistas.

It is a world that is not only beautiful because it is eternal, but because it eternally grows in beauty. And magically, as you grow more beautiful from within, the outer world soon begins to change in marvelous ways as well. Everything changes before your very eyes. You gain a new outlook. You begin to weave straw into gold. Turn a sow's ear into silk. Make lemonade from lemons. Because God has revealed His secrets to you.

The only way to change your outer world is to change your inner world.

Make it a garden!

If you would like to learn more
about the Science of Correspondences
and the spiritual discoveries of Emanuel Swedenborg,
please contact:

Swedenborg Foundation
320 N. Church Street
West Chester, PA 19380
(800) 355-3222
http://www.swedenborg.com/
(email) info@swedenborg.com

INDEX

A

Acceptance, 44
Acknowledge, 93
Act of goodness, 46
Actions
    emanates from, 104
    leave a taste, 46
    proper, 74
Adam, 39
    representing the understanding, 99-102
    see humus
    see ground
Adam and Eve, 5, 22, 33, 96, 99-102
Aesop's fables, 73
Aim, 48, 97
    original goal, 63
    aimlessness, 93
Analogies, 4, 17, 30, 33, 86
    analogous to, 13, 66, 68, 70
Ancient
    civilizations, 4
    formula, 15
    legend, 7, 84, *footnote*, 5
    Persian word for, 5
    philosophers, 5
    Science of Correspondences, 5-6
Ancients, 7
Anger, 67, 73, 82
    lose temper, 68
Animal kingdom, 28, 72-75, 96-98
Animals, 41, 43, 87-88, 96-99, 101
    critters, 73, 79
    critter heaven, 97
    interconnectedness with, 106
    of Noah's Ark, 73
    portray human qualities, 73
    stuffed, 73
Appetites
    kingdom of, 73
    personal, 62
    primitive, 82
    see animal kingdom
Apple
    bad apples, 102
    Forbidden Fruit, 101-102
    see fruit
Appropriate, 94
Artifical
    contrivance, 70
    methods, 49-51
    principles, 30-31, 35
    solutions, *footnote*, 83
Artifciality
    lifestyles, 29
    limited scope, 30, *footnote*, 83
    of modern world, 3

B

Artificial fertilizers, 22-23, 29-31
    see chemicals
Asvattha tree
    footnote, 42

Babel, Tower of, 35
Balance, 3, 6, 82, 85, 87, 99, 104
Baptism, 16
Battleground
    within each of us, 110
    see tribulation
Beast of the Apocalypse, 110
Beasts, 96, 98, 101
    see animals
Beaten path, 33, 77
Beauty
    eternal, 111
    harmonious activity, 106
    in spiritual ideas, 81
    of inner garden, 44
    physical, 3
    too many beautiful things, 103
Beliefs, 28, 35, 39, 61
Belief system, 42, 69
    see faith
    see principles
Benefit to all, 13, 104
    of the ecosystem, 13
Bhagavad-gita, 94, 104
Bible, 12, 33, 37, 62
Big picture, 13, 31, 35, 107
Bind
    into a coherent whole, 35
    meaning of religion, *footnote*, 37
Birds
    of prey, 83-84
    feather, *footnote*, 100
    represent, 81, 83
    winged fowl, *biblical passage*, 81
Biomass, 86
Blossom
    ideas, 4, 44, 71
    our inner gardens, 62
    unselfish thoughts, 104
Bodily kingdom, 43
    cellular anarchy, 85
    death of, 91
    purpose of organs, 107
Body of knowledge, 16
Born anew
    biblical passage, 91
    reborn, 109
Brain
    inquisitive, 61

Hell, 45
Help
from above, 52, 66, 85
helpful instruction, 43
outside, 64, 66
from God, 68
Herbs, medicinal, 40-43
Hinduism, *footnote*, 42
Hierarchy of values, 88
Hieroglyphs
footnotes, 5, 99
see Science of Correspondences
Homer
The Odyssey, *footnote*, 62
Horror movies, 28, 84
Humility, 13, 32, 37-39, 52, 69
hasten development of, 92
humbling, 39, 93
true, 111
Humus, 13, 30, 36-39, 92-93, 111

I

Ideas
bear fruit, 97
break down, 93
distilled from memory, 81, 86
draw upon, 83
lay to rest, 92
more organized, 87-88
species of, 80
superior, 62
that swim, 104
Imagination, 80, 83, 89, 104
Indians, 16
Information Age, 18
see flood, memory
Inner conflict, 104, 109-110
enemies, 110
see tribulations
Insects, represent, 82-83
annoying pests, 7
emotional pests, 69
gone from the inner garden, 104
Interdependence
between plants and animals, 99, 106
Internet, 17
Introspection, 93
see compost pile
Islamic teaching, 92
Israelites, 32

J

Jonah, 84
Judgement, 41, 66
clouds judgement, 49

fruits of labors can be judged, 101
misjudgement, 48, 85
support of, 99

K

Karma, 52
Knowing
the truth and oneself, 67
Knowledge
artificial contrivance, 70
knowledge of commandments, 72
must develop first, 74
pattern our, 80
self knowledge, 67-68
spiritual, 83
useful, 80
to feed cleverness, 51
value system organizes, 34
see artificial chemicals, education, water,
memory

L

Legends, 5, 7, 84
Light, 95
a light that opens, 10
appear in good light, 51
continuous source of, 61, 68
from above, 66
inner light, 10
insights received from, 25
let there be, 9, 11-12, 38
light bulb, 9-10, 25
of God's truth, 66, 103
of understanding, 12, 62
seeing the light, 11-12, 14, 71
see enlightenment
Lord's return, 108-109
His promise, 109
Love
definition of, 107
energizes every aspect, 71
exaltation of, 108
expand shere of, 13, 90
God's Circle of, 108
highest position, 88
hierarchy of, 88-89
labor of, 98
lovers, 70
loves to love, 104
makes truth organic, 71
one's neighbor, 12-13, 90
source of warmth, 69-71, 95, 98
towards others, 91
true love, 3
warmth of God's love, 103

118

M

Mammals
  signifies, 98
  Manger, *footnote*, 73
Man, fall of, 88
  represents understanding, 99-102
Marriage
  between understanding and will, 99-102
Memory, 16-17, 25, 41, 72, 80-81, 83-84, 86, 104
  remind yourself, 63
Mind, 1
  becomes more fertile, 87
  constantly mixing, 86
  evolved equally with, 98-99
  from the mind to the heart, 71, 89
  is fed directly, 50
  love opens our minds, 70
  more than memory, 72
  new dimensions of activity, 72-75, 81-82
  Nor can it grow without, 64
  obscurred, 109
  paradise for, 61
  presence of, 67
  should not be in servitude to, 85
Mineral kingdom, 27-52, 72, 88
  see principles
Monsters, 28, 84
Mother Nature, 52
  speeding up the forces of, 92
Muhammed, 91
Mythology, Greek, 85

N

Nature
  analogous to, 88, 106
  as teacher, 24
  as soil becomes more fertile, 87
  balance of, 82, 99
  complex relationships, 23-24, 106
  evolves towards harmony, 94
  increased activity of, 70, 75
  Nature of man, 86-95, 106
  Nature's wisdom, 12, 85
  speeding up the forces of, 92
  the higher forms in, 84
  the world of, 72
  Unlike Nature, 83
  Workings of, 86
Neurosis, 99
New evaluation, 10-11
New Jerusalem
  biblical passage, 94
Nirvana, 103
  true nature of, 106
Noah's Ark, 17-18, 73

O

Objectivity, 67, 81-82
  highest or widest view, 85, 89, 104
  see limited scope
Obscurity, 12
  see clouds, void
Obstacles, 12
  opposition, 64
  see challenges, tribulations
Order, 36-37, 85-89
  against true order, 83
  of the ecosystem, 87
  reversal of, 84, 88
Organic
  definition of, 107
  life, 72
Organic matter, 24, 36-37
  see humus, humility
Organic processes
  of intellectual growth, 86-88
Organizing power, 36, 39, 80, 85, 107
  reorganizes, 86
  see hierarchy of values

P

Parables, *footnote*, 5
Paradise, 5, 61, 96, 103-104, 108
  paradisiacal vision, 75
Perfection through diversity, 106
Personal demons, 110
Pharaoh, 32
Phoenix, the, 90
Plant kingdom, 28, 72
  analogous to thoughts, 74, 87-88
  corresponds to intellectual world, 41
  flowers represent, 44
  herbs correspond to, 43
  interconnectedness of, 106
  noxious plants of inner garden, 42
  plants in the inner garden, 40
  see seeds, fruit, belief systems, faith
Ponce de Leon, 16
Principles
  all true principles, 36
  artificial, 35
  causes our, 88
  challenged, 66
  conflicting, 24
  different, 29
  heavenly, 108
  higher, 32
  organic, 35-36, 40, 74
  rooted in, 40, 48, 69
  solidifies his, 27

Designed & photographed by Susan Sylvia
Text set in Raleigh, 11 on 13 with ragged right
Headings in Pompeii Capitals
Italics in Novarese Book Italic